Contents

Foreword

This textbook has been structured so that students studying the Short and Full Courses in GCSE ICT can easily make use of it. There are common elements that relate to both specifications. Those elements which relate to the **Full course only** have been identified using a pink bar along the side of the page. All other material should be covered by students studying any of the two courses (Short or Full).

Within the coursework section (C1) there is reference to electronic files which support the practical exercises. These can be found at www.hoddernorthernireland.co.uk/ict/ .

This material can be downloaded and used to assist in the development of practical skills. Completing the exercises will give students the skills required to complete the coursework elements of the specification.

Further exemplar material for some of the assignments can also be found on the website. This material is intended to give students a preview of how finished assignments might be presented.

1 Web browser packages

> **In this section you will learn about web browsers.**
> **Through examples you will gain skills which will assist in:**
> - opening an Internet site
> - using a search engine to carry out simple and complex searches
> - organising favourites/bookmarks
>
> **This is assessed through the following components:**
> - Terminal examination(s)
> - Assignment A2: Produce a booklet or report
> - Assignment A3: Design a website
> - Assignment B1: Using the Internet

Opening an Internet site

This section is supported by the following digital media which may be accessed through www.hoddernorthern ireland.co.uk/ict/ MyFavouriteBandsB1 – Word Document

The World Wide Web (WWW) consists of a vast number of pages provided by individuals, organisations and businesses. When the pages are grouped together they form a website and the first page on a website is known as the home page. Most websites contain pages in multimedia format as they consist of a mixture of words, sound, video, images and animation. Pages on a website are linked together using hypertext links. Hypertext refers to keywords highlighted in a different colour or graphics that, when clicked on, move from page to page or website to website. The cursor normally changes from a pointer to a hand when it recognises a hypertext link. Each website has its own unique address.

■ Website addresses

A website will have its own unique identification or address. The website address is formally called an Uniform Resource Locator (URL). Consider the URL http://www.bbc.co.uk

▶ **URL component parts**

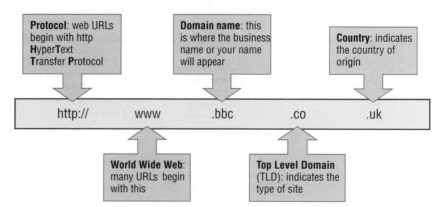

Protocol: web URLs begin with http **H**yper**T**ext **T**ransfer **P**rotocol

Domain name: this is where the business name or your name will appear

Country: indicates the country of origin

http://   www   .bbc   .co   .uk

World Wide Web: many URLs begin with this

Top Level Domain (TLD): indicates the type of site

You may see different references to top level domain names. Although there are many domain names used, the table below shows some of the common ones.

Top level domain	Meaning
.co	Indicates a company
.com	A commercial organisation
.org	Reference to a charity or non-profit organisation
.ac	Reference to a university or college
.sch	Reference to a school
.net	Reference to a network

■ Web browser

Many ICT users refer to the phrase *surfing the net*. A web browser is a software package that allows access to the Internet. Most computers use Microsoft Internet Explorer as their web browser, but Netscape Navigator is also a web browser. The following diagram shows the features of a typical browser.

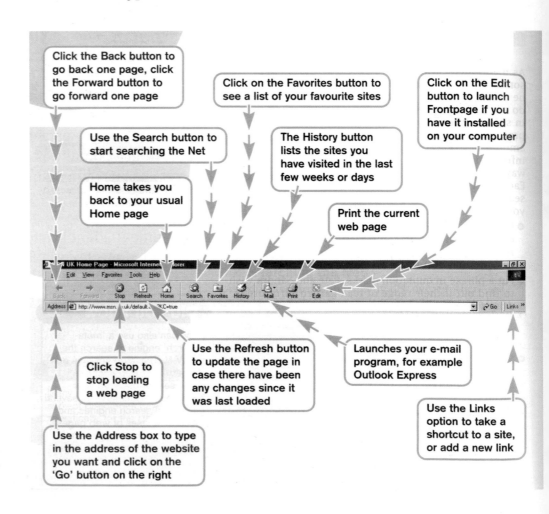

Click the Back button to go back one page, click the Forward button to go forward one page

Click on the Favorites button to see a list of your favourite sites

Click on the Edit button to launch Frontpage if you have it installed on your computer

Use the Search button to start searching the Net

The History button lists the sites you have visited in the last few weeks or days

Home takes you back to your usual Home page

Print the current web page

Click Stop to stop loading a web page

Use the Refresh button to update the page in case there have been any changes since it was last loaded

Launches your e-mail program, for example Outlook Express

Use the Links option to take a shortcut to a site, or add a new link

Use the Address box to type in the address of the website you want and click on the 'Go' button on the right

■ Using a search engine to carry out simple and complex searches

These browsers also use Internet search engines which allow the user to enter keywords and phrases to find information quickly. Each search engine maintains a large database of websites. There are many search engines available such as:

- Google
- Ask Jeeves
- Excite
- Lycos
- Alta Vista
- Yahoo!
- Metacrawler
- Northern Light
- Go

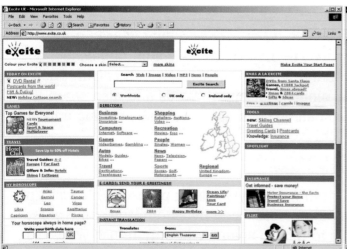

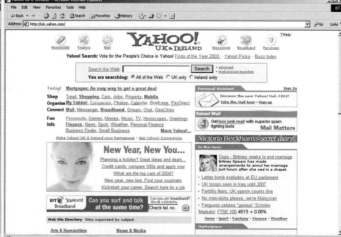

Most search engines, such as Google and Yahoo!, include an advanced search facility for the more experienced users.

Google Advanced Search

Find results	with **all** of the words		10 results	Google Search
	with the **exact phrase**		
	with **at least one** of the words	
	without the words	
Language	Return pages written in	English
File Format	Only ▾ return results of the file format	any format ▾
Date	Return web pages updated in the	anytime ▾
Occurrences	Return results where my terms occur	anywhere in the page ▾
Domain	Only ▾ return results from the site or domain	e.g. google.com, .org More info
SafeSearch	⦿ No filtering ○ Filter using SafeSearch	

YAHOO! Search UK & IRELAND

You'll find it on eBay

Advanced Web Search

Find web pages

include all of the words:	music festival*
include this exact phrase:	
include at least one of these words:	
exclude these words:	

Start the Search

More Options

Language:	only show pages in	English ▾
Country:	only show pages from	United Kingdom ▾
Date:	only show pages updated in the	past 3 months ▾
Keyword Locations:	show pages where the keyword is	anywhere in the page ▾
Domain:	Only ▾ show pages from the site or domain	
		e.g., yahoo.com, .org, .gov

Start the Search

■ Searching techniques

It is important to employ a number of techniques when using a search engine. Inexperienced users tend to type a phrase into the text box provided by the search engine. You should consider some of the following techniques.

Using capital and small letters

When you enter keywords and phrases in small letters, the search engine will return websites that consist of both lower and uppercase versions of websites.

Using wildcards

The asterisk (*) can help searching. It acts as a character in a keyword. For example, entering Schoo* returns websites containing *school* or *schools* or *schooling*. Entering Colo*r returns *color* and *colour*. Therefore it is best used for finding singular or plural words and also when a word may have different spelling such as an English spelling and an American spelling.

Quotation marks

Using quotation marks (" ") around keywords or phrases will assist in more exact searches including words side by side in the same order. For example, "apartments to rent in spain" will only return websites matching this phrase exactly.

Keywords first!

Using good grammar is important when writing in English. However, for a search, when you decide on a suitable phrase, it is not important to type it using standard grammar. If you list the words in the phrase in order of importance it will lead to a better search. For example, if you want to search for websites that allow you to choose a dog breed that would be suitable as a family pet you may enter the search as – dog breed family pet choose. This means the search will initially focus on dogs.

Plus (+) and minus (−)

Using the plus and minus signs in front of keywords allows the user to force inclusion or exclusion from phrases. For example, the phrase spain +cities −madrid will return websites referencing all Spanish cities except Madrid. Therefore entering the phrase revision +GCSE −history will return websites that refer to GCSE revision in subjects except history.

Complex logic

This involves using AND, OR and NOT

school AND pupil
 [returns websites that contain both *school* and *pupil*]

school OR pupil
 [returns websites that contain either *school* or *pupil*]

school NOT pupil
 [returns websites that contain *school* but not *pupil*]

■ Example of using a variety of searching techniques

Consider a situation where you invite your friends around to your house for dinner. You are told that most of them are vegetarians and one of them is celebrating their birthday. You then decide to use the Internet to search for vegetarian recipes for special occasions.
 You plan the following searches:

Search	Comments on search
vegetarian	One keyword will return millions of websites, making the search ineffective.
vegetarian AND recipe	Websites must include both keywords, therefore it narrows the search.
vegetarian AND recipe*	Returns websites where recipe and recipes (singular and plural) occur, therefore widening the search.
(vegetarian OR vegan) AND (recipe*)	Returns websites that include vegetarian and recipe* or vegan and recipe*, therefore widening the search
(vegetarian OR veggie OR vegan) AND (recipe* OR cook*) AND ("special occasion*")	Narrows website hits as the phrase *special occasion* or *special occasions* must be in each website.

When setting up a search on the Internet you should follow some simple guidelines including:

■ Always do a plan.
■ Build a simple initial search, usually one or two keywords, and test it.
■ Add one refinement at a time to a copy of the previous working search and perform the search.

■ Organising favourites and bookmarks

Double clicking on the Internet Explorer icon will display your homepage:

If you enter a website address in the address box, such as www.schoolzone.co.uk, the home page of that website will normally appear on the screen.

If you find this website useful you can add it to your favourites which means you do not have to remember the address each time.

Select the menu **Favorites** and the option **Add to Favorites** . . . .

If you are happy with the name reference in the dialog box, press **OK**.

After using Internet for a while, you will begin to build a list of your favourite websites. This list can be organised into folders to make reference and searching easier.

Select **Favorites** and the option **Organize Favorites** . . . .

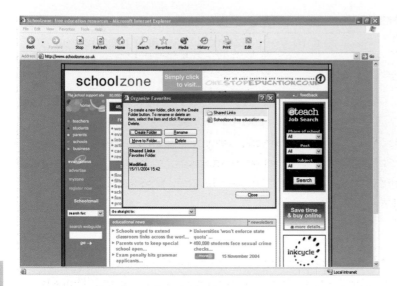

The dialog box **Organize Favorites** will appear.

Advice on producing coursework assignment using the Internet

◼ Overall presentation

It is important to include:

- a front cover indicating clearly your Centre number and Candidate number
- the title of the topic chosen and a relevant graphic illustrating your topic
- Activity 1 and Activity 2 separately.

◼ Activity 1

Select a topic from a subject you are currently studying. You should produce a plan of relevant words, concepts, narrower and broader terms, synonyms and date span, etc. Decide on the search engine. You are only required to use one search engine but you must be able to give reasons for your choice.

From the websites you select, you must download the material (text and graphics) you need and explain why the material was relevant to your research. For example, you could download text into a wordprocessing package. It is important to show how you integrate the text with the graphics from the different websites.

After you download all the relevant information required you must create a table to evaluate three of the websites used in your assignment. Before creating the table you should decide on appropriate criteria that could become column headings in your table. Typical column headings could be:

- Search engine used
- Website/URL address
- Picture of homepage
- Information found
- Good points
- Bad points
- Links to other websites
- Accessibility
- Rating (1 to 10).

When you have created your table you need to use your email account and send your table as an attachment to your teacher with appropriate use of email skills. It would also be a good idea to get a printout of your teacher's email inbox as evidence of having sent the email.

■ Activity 2

In this section you must include key evidence of your searches including your refinements, downloading and integrating your text and graphics found. There is no need to produce a large essay-type document on the topic researched. It would be advisable to describe how some of the downloaded material (text and graphics) was integrated and laid out, and to explain how you refined your searches using screen dumps from the search engine(s) used.

2 Web creation software C1(b)

▶ **In this section you will learn about using a web design package and designing a website.**
Through the worked example you will gain skills which will assist in:

- designing a website
- using background colour or design
- including graphics
- creating links to pages and other websites
- including animation, sound and video

▶ **This is assessed through the following components:**

- Terminal Examination
- Assignment A3: Design a website

This section is supported by the following digital media which may be accessed through www.hoddernorthern ireland.co.uk/ict/
These are the files and folders you will require.

■ Some features of a web design package

Feature	Explanation
HTML pages	All web creation tools allow users to create HyperText Markup Language pages. This is the language used for web pages.
Hyperlinks	A hyperlink is a picture or text which when clicked links the user to another web page. All web creation tools allow users to create links.
Different views of the webpage	A web designer can look at the web pages in design view, in HTML view or in preview mode. HTML view will show the language only. Design view lets the user add text and pictures to the page. Preview mode opens the page in a web browser and lets the user see what it will look like when open on the WWW.
Navigation	Web creation tools manage the navigation layout of the website. This is shown as a picture, indicating how each page is linked to the other pages in the website.
Tables	Tables can be added to web pages. Most packages have a tables option and the table properties can be set.
Frameset	A frameset is a group of pages which can be set up as one page. The frameset may have a left-hand page and a top page as well as the main page for text. Although each page is saved separately the frameset makes the pages look like a single page in a web browser.
Text	Web creation tools allow different fonts, styles, colours and effects to be selected for text.
Pictures	Pictures can be included in web pages and some packages have a picture toolbar which allows the designer to edit the picture from within the web page.

■ Consider the following scenario

John attends a local drama school. He has been asked by the director of the drama school to design a website which will publicise the school, classes and activities in the local community.

After discussion with the director, John suggests including the following pages:

- A home page, which is the first page people will see. The home page will connect to all other pages.
- A page about the classes that are available.
- A page about the special events that go on during the year.
- A page about fund raising activities and links with the local community.
- A page containing details about grades that can be taken and when they can be taken during the year.
- A news page for class members.

John uses a page layout diagram to show the director how the pages will look.

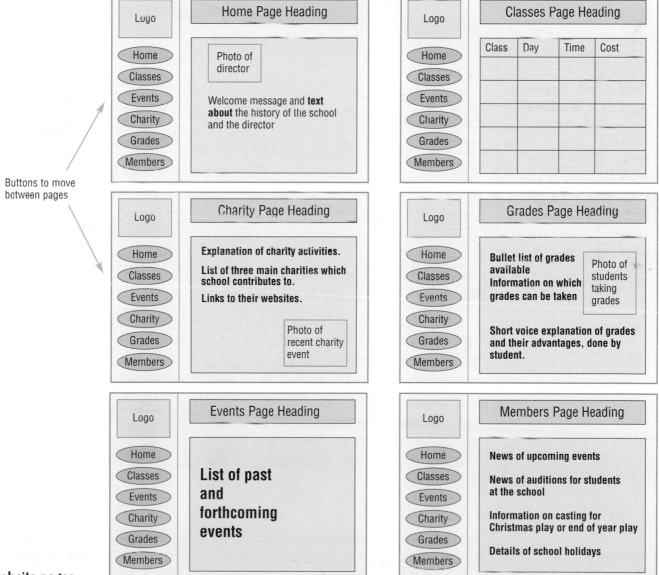

Buttons to move between pages

▶ **Website pages**

John has not decided on any animation or the font or colour scheme he will use in the website. Now that he knows how the webpages will be laid out he can begin to think about the colours and fonts.

It is clear from his web pages that each page will have the same border on the left-hand side. This will contain the navigation buttons so that users can go from one page to another.

How to create a website using a web design tool – Microsoft FrontPage

Open FrontPage and you will see the **Page** view window.

Click the views toolbar to see your website in different views

The tabs allow you to see your web pages in normal format, HTML format or a preview of what the page looks like on the WWW.

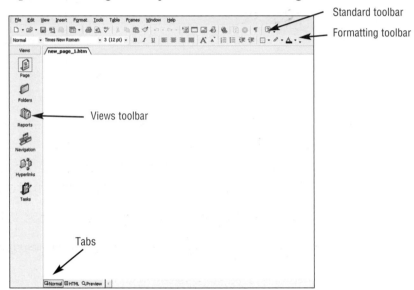

Standard toolbar

Formatting toolbar

Views toolbar

Tabs

■ How to create a website

A website is a set of HTML documents which you can view on the World Wide Web. The documents are usually linked together using *hyperlinks.* HyperText Markup Language (HTML) is the language which is used to create web pages. Most web design packages generate the HTML for you. Some people still write the HTML themselves and then view the pages using a browser. A hyperlink is a piece of text or a picture which when clicked will link to another webpage.

In John's website, the buttons down the side of the pages will be hyperlinks.

To create a website in FrontPage:

1 Click on the arrow next to the **New page** button and click Web... .
2 On the **Web Sites** tab on the new dialog box, click on *Empty Web*.
3 Give the website the name *Johns Website*.
4 Click OK.

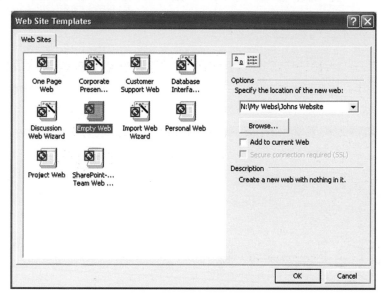

5 Click on Navigation on the **Views** menu. There are no pages in the website at present so click on the new page icon ▫ to add a page.

6 Right click on the home page and rename it *Homepage.*

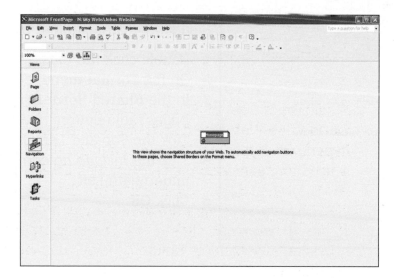

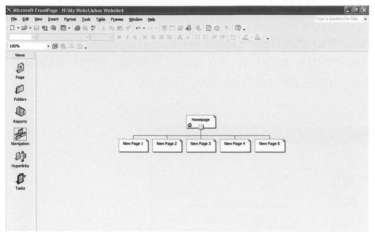

7 To add the five other pages in the website, click the home page and then click ▢ five times.

8 Right click on each page and and rename each one as follows:
- New Page 1 – Classes
- New Page 2 – Events
- New Page 3 – Charity
- New Page 4 – Grades
- New Page 5 – Members

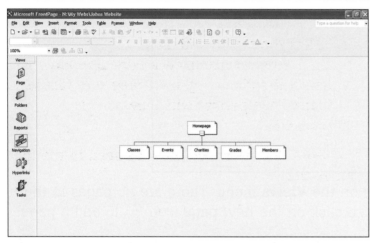

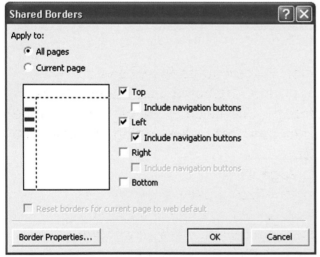

■ Adding navigation to the website

Navigation can be added by using shared borders.

1 Double click the *Classes* page.
2 On the **Format** menu, click **Shared Borders**... .
3 In the **Shared Borders** dialog box click the *All pages* radio button.
4 Tick the *Top* and *Left* check boxes.
5 Tick the *Include navigation buttons* check box underneath Left.
6 Click **OK**.

Your page will appear as follows:

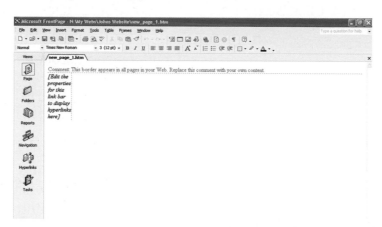

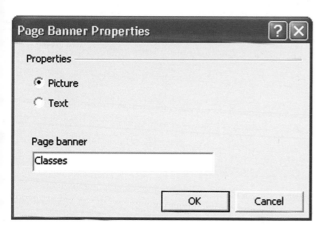

7   Select the top shared area.
8   On the **Insert** menu, click *Page Banner...* .
9   Select the Picture option. Make sure Classes is the Page banner text shown.
10 Click **OK**.

The word Classes should now be seen in the top shared area.

Adding a navigation bar to the left-hand side

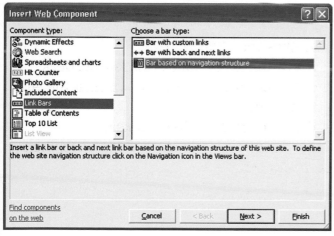

1   Click on *Folders* in the **Views** menu.
2   Right click on **Homepage** and select *Set* as homepage. The name of the page will change to index.htm This makes setting up navigation easier.
3   Go to **Page** view.
4   Open the Classes page.
5   Click in the left shared border area.
6   On the **Insert** menu, click *Navigation*.
7   The **Insert Web Component** window will appear.
8   Choose *Link Bars* from the **Component type** window.
9   Choose *Bar based on navigation structure* from the **Choose a bar type** window.

10 Select *Use Page's Theme* from the **Choose a bar style** window.

11 Click **Next**.

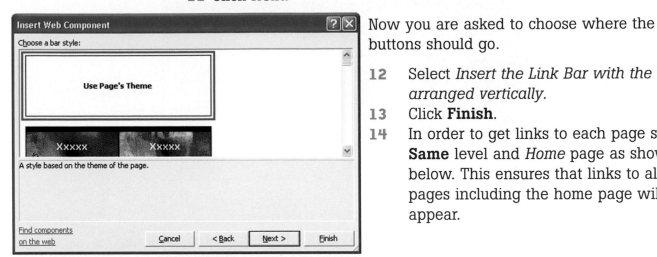

Now you are asked to choose where the buttons should go.

12 Select *Insert the Link Bar with the links arranged vertically.*

13 Click **Finish**.

14 In order to get links to each page select **Same** level and *Home* page as shown below. This ensures that links to all pages including the home page will appear.

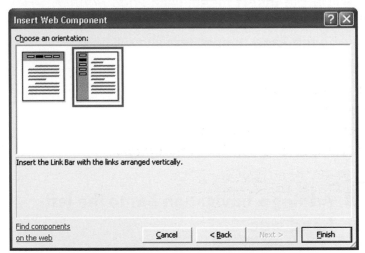

Your page will look like this:

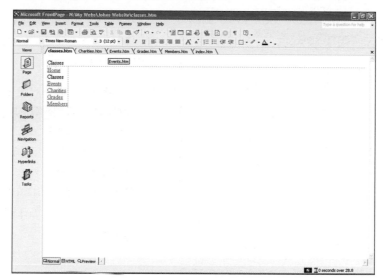

Setting up navigation for the Home page of the website is done separately.

1 Click on *index.htm*.
2 Right click on the left shared border.
3 Select **Link bar properties**... .
4 Choose the *Child pages under Home* option.
5 Click the *Home Page* check box under *Additional pages*:

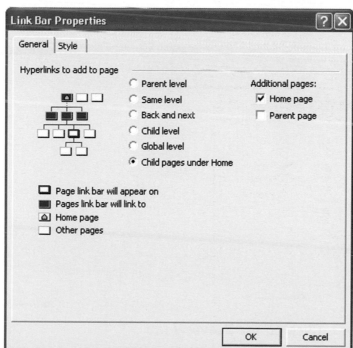

Now you have a website structure. Save your website structure.

6 From the **File** menu select *Save All*.

■ Giving the website a colour scheme and buttons

The next task is to make the website look good. A theme can be applied.

1 Go to the classes page.
2 From the **Format** menu select *Theme...* .

3 Select the *Watermark* theme.
4 Click on the *All pages* radio button to make sure the theme is applied to all of the web pages.
5 Tick the *Vivid colors* check box to make the colours slightly brighter.
6 Click **OK**.

The Classes page will look like this:

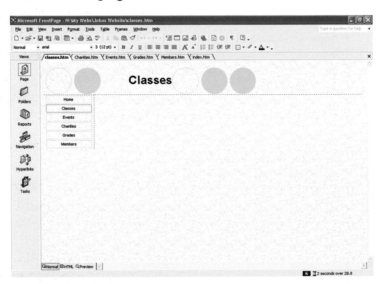

7 Click on the **Preview** tab.

When the page is previewed, Classes looks like this (note that the links do not work here).

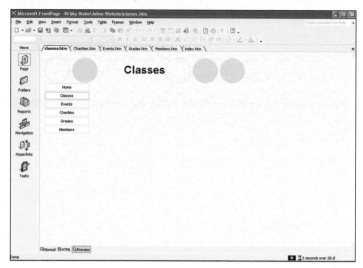

To check all of the links in the website:

■ From the **File** menu, select *Preview in browser… .*

The webpage will open in the selected browser and the links can be checked.

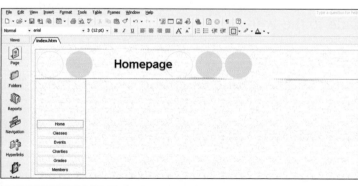

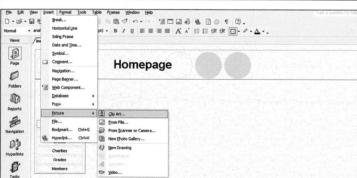

■ Placing content into the website

The website needs to have the information placed in the correct places. A logo still has to be placed at the top of the navigation buttons. This means making a change to the left shared border. Any changes made to this area in one page will be made in every other page automatically. A logo can be inserted as follows:

1 Go to index.htm and open the page in **Page** view.
2 Click on the left shared border.
3 Add three blank lines above the home button.

Now insert the logo.

4 From the **Insert** menu, select *Picture.*

Now select the location where the logo will come from. A picture can be inserted from clip art, from a file, scanner, camera or video using this method.

5 Insert the picture which is to be used for the logo.

The picture used in this website is available in a document called websitefile.doc on the website www.hodder northernireland.co.uk/ict/. It can be copied and pasted from this document into position on the webpage.

■ Making the picture transparent on the webpage

1 Click on the picture, the **Pictures toolbar** will appear.
2 Click on the **Set Transparent Color** icon.
3 Move the cursor onto the picture.
4 Click on the white background of the picture. The picture should now become transparent.

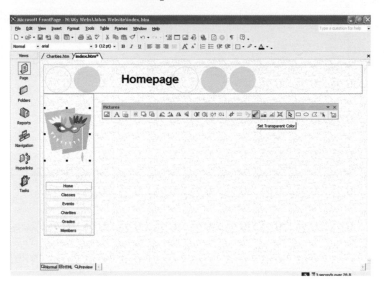

5 Preview the webpage.
6 Save the changes made to the website.

■ Changing the page headings

It is useful to see the pages in the website alongside the page view. To do this:

1 From the **View** menu, select *Folder List*.
2 Page view will now appear like this:

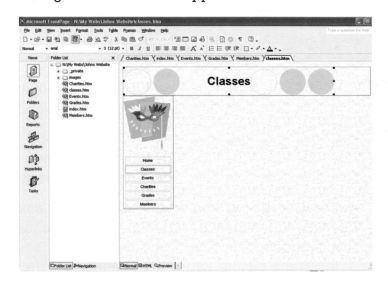

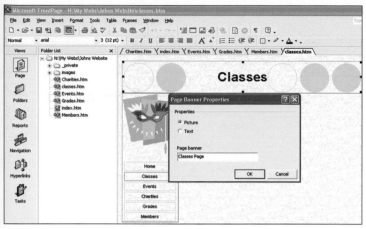

3 To access each page **double click** on it in the Folder List.
4 Go to the classes page.
5 Double click in the Classes page banner.

6 Change the Page Banner to *Classes Page*. The Classes page will appear as follows.
8 Change the Page Banners in the other pages as follows:
   ● *Index.htm* – Welcome to Acting It Out.
   ● *Events.htm* – Events September – June.

Inserting a table into the Classes page

1 Open the Classes page.
2 Place the cursor in the main area of the page (not in any of the shared borders).
3 From the **Insert** menu, select *Table*. The Insert Table dialogue box will appear.
4 Set the table properties as follows.

This means the table will have 6 rows, 4 columns and the cell borders will be visible on the page.

This table is available in the file websitefile.doc at www.hoddernorthern ireland.co.uk/ict/

5 Place the following information into the table.

Class	Day	Time	Cost
Primary 1	Monday	3.30pm	£3.50
Primary 2 & 3	Monday	4.30pm	£3.50
Primary 4	Monday	5.30pm	£3.50
Primary 5	Wednesday	3.30pm	£4.00
Primary 6	Wednesday	4.30pm	£4.00
Primary 7	Wednesday	5.30pm	£4.00
Age 11–13	Wednesday	6:45pm	£4.50
Age 14–16	Saturday	2.00pm	£6.00

6 Centre the *Time* and *Cost* column headings.

7 Centre the contents of the *Time* and *Cost* columns.

8 Right click anywhere in the table. The Table Properties will appear.

9 Set the height of the cells to 250 pixels as shown.

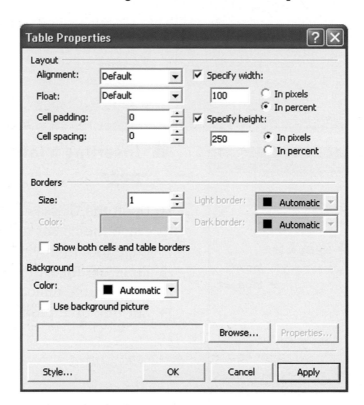

10 Click **Apply**.

11 Click **OK**.

11 Save the changes made to the Classes Page.

> Alternatively you may copy and paste the text from the file websitefile.doc

■ Inserting text into the Grades page

1 Open the Grades page.
2 Enter the following text.

The following grades are available at Acting It Out:

- Grade 1 for ages 8–9
- Grade 2 for ages 9–10
- Grade 3 for ages 10–11
- Grade 4 for ages 11–12
- Grade 5 for ages 12–13

- Grade 6 for ages 13–14
- Grade 7 for ages 14–15
- Grade 8 for ages 15–16
- Teacher's Diploma for Post-16

All pupils prepare for grades from January until June. Each pupil must produce a portfolio in advance of the grade examination. The portfolio is sent to the examining body. Visiting examiners interview and test each pupil individually on the content of their portfolio. Pupils are expected to recite the contents of their portfolio at grades 1–6.

3 Highlight all of the bullets points and make them *italic*.
4 Save the Grades page.

■ Adding sound to the Grades page

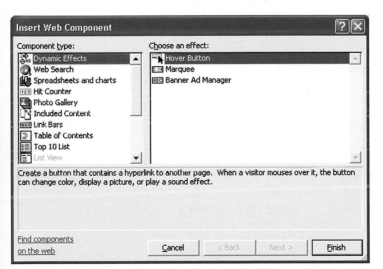

1 Copy the sound *Student.wav* from the website www.awebsite.com.
2 Place the sound into the web folder *Johns Website.*
3 Copy the file *gradestudent.jpg* from the website to the folder *Johns Website.*
4 From the **Insert** menu, select *Web component.* The Insert Web Component dialog box will appear.
5 Select *Dynamic Effects* from the **Component type**: list.
6 Select *Hover Button* from the **Choose an effect**: list.
7 Set the Hover Button Properties as shown.
8 Browse to the file list and select *Student.wav* from the list.
9 Click **OK**.
10 From the **File** menu, select *Preview in browser.*

At this point a question about the media player being used may be asked.

11 Select the correct media player and click **OK**.

12 Click on the Student button and listen to the student.

When a hover button is added to the website some new files are placed in the folder list.

■ Inserting a picture beside the text on the Grades page

1 From the **Table** menu, select *Insert Table*.

2 Insert a table with one row and two columns as shown.

3 Set the border of the table to 0. This means that the table borders will not be visible to users of the website.

4 Highlight the bullet point text about the grades.

5 Cut the text.

6 Paste the text into the first cell in the table.

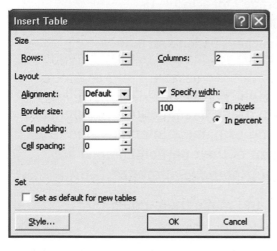

7 Go to the next cell.

8 From the **Insert** menu, select *Picture*.

9 Select *From file* and browse to the picture *gradestudent.jpg*.

10 Click *Open*.

11 You may resize the picture if you wish.

12 Save *Charities.htm*.

13 Preview the page and note that the table is not visible.

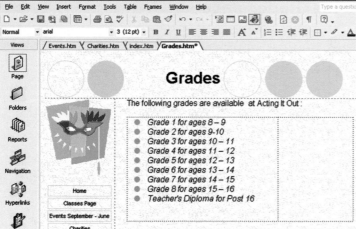

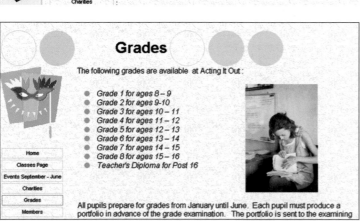

> Alternatively you can copy and paste it from the file websitefile.doc

■ Inserting text into the home page

1 Open the file index.htm.
2 Insert the following text into the home page.

"Hello and welcome to the Acting It Out website. We hope that this website will give you some information on what we do at our school as well as an understanding of the school's principles.

Acting It Out was founded by myself, Edward Black, in 2001. I felt that giving young people an opportunity to learn about performing arts would contribute to their personal development and for some might lead to a career in acting. The school offers classes for all age groups and pupils at the school are prepared for grades each year. The school enters many pupils for auditions for local shows and films and to date we have had a lot of success.

Our pupils participate in fundraising activities as a way of contributing to their local community who support our performances so well. You are welcome to come to our premises at 23 Longsdale Road to find out more.

Thank you
Edward Black

email edwardblack@actingitout.com | Tel: 0983458666 | Fax: 0983458667 | Address: 23 Longsdale Road"

3 Save the file *index.htm*.
4 Preview the file in the browser.

■ Adding a picture of the director to the home page

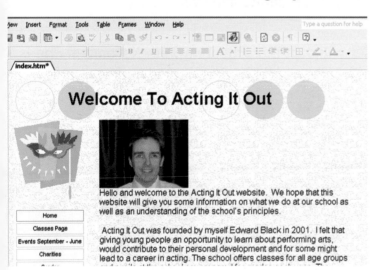

1 Copy the picture *director.jpg* to the folder Johns Website. The file is available on the website *www.hoddernorthernireland.co. uk/ict/*.
2 From the **Insert** menu select *Picture*.
3 Select *From File... .*
4 Browse to the file called *director.jpg*.
5 Click *Open*.
6 Position the picture at the top of the page.
7 Save the file *index.htm*.
8 Preview the page.

■ Making the email address work

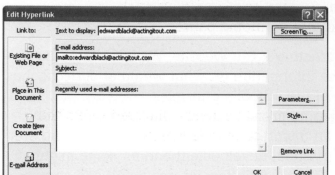

1 Select the email address text.
2 Right click and select hyperlink properties.
3 Enter the text shown in the email address.
4 Save *index.htm*.

> Alternatively you can copy and paste it from the file websitefile.doc

■ Inserting text into the Members page

1 Open the file *Members.htm*.
2 Insert the following text into the Members page.

"Welcome to our members' page. This page is designed to keep all class members up to date on what is happening at Acting It Out.

Current activities

Christmas rehearsals are ongoing and will be held in the theatre for the next three weeks.

All fees for grades should be submitted in an envelope with your name on the front by 25th January.

Auditions

Congratulations to three of our pupils Andrea Wilkins, Michael Darcy and Ellen Green who have successfully auditioned for the local film 'Wake Up Call'.

A commercial advertiser will visit the school on 29th November. She is looking for three teenagers to model shows in an advertisement for Clarks Shoes."

3 Organise the information so that it fits on one screen.
4 Make the words *Current activities* and *Auditions* bold.
5 Save the Members page.
6 Preview the page.

■ Inserting information into the Events page

1 Open the file *Events.htm.*
2 Insert a table into the page. The table should have 6 rows and 3 columns.
3 Select the entire table and set the row height to 300.

A similar task was completed when the Classes page was created.

The cells in the third column must be merged. To do this:

4 Select the cells in the third column.
5 Right click and select *Merge Cells.*

6 Make the first two columns slightly narrower and the third column wider. To do this click on the column border line and drag it along.
7 Enter the information as follows.

Alternatively you can copy and paste it from the file websitefile.doc

Event	Month	
Class Fees	October	
Christmas Show	December	
Fund Raising Day	February	
Regional Drama Festival	March	
Grades	June	

■ Inserting a picture into the Events page with a picture swap behaviour

1 Open *Events.htm*.
2 From the **Insert** menu, select *Picture*.
3 Select *From File... .*
4 Browse to the file called *Angel.jpg*.
5 Click Open.
6 Resize this picture so that it fits into the third column.
7 Select the picture.
8 From the **Format** menu, select *Dynamic HTML Effects*.
9 Select **Mouse Over** from the *On* drop-down list.
10 Select **Swap Picture** from the *Apply* drop-down list.
11 Click on **Choose picture** and browse to the picture *dressedup.jpg*.

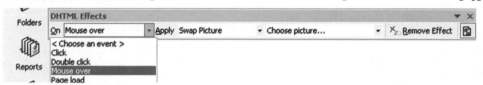

12 Preview your page.

The pictures on the page should swap when the mouse is rolled over them.

■ Inserting text and hyperlinks into the Charities page

Edward has talked to John about the Charities page. He thinks it is a good idea to have a link to the website of each charity that they support.

Alternatively you can copy and paste it from the file www.hoddernorthern ireland.co.uk/ict/

1 Insert the following text into the Charities page.

"Our Favourite Charities are:

National Society for Prevention of Cruelty to Children
Last year we donated £350.00 to the NSPCC.
Save the Children
Last year we donated £130.00 to the Save the Children charity.
World Wildlife Fund
Last year we donated £120.00 to the WWF.

Please visit the websites of our favourite charities. You can see the good work that they do. You could even make a donation."

2 Make the names of each charity bold.

Making hyperlinks to the charity websites

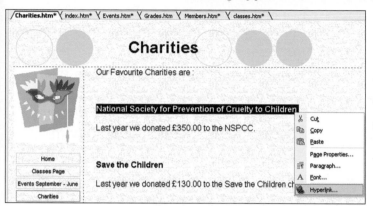

3 Select the text *National Society for Prevention of Cruelty to Children.*
4 Right click on the text.
5 Select *Hyperlink... .*

The Insert Hyperlink dialog box will appear.

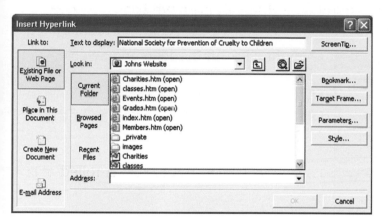

6 In the address box enter *www.nspcc.org.uk.*
7 Click on Screen Tip
8 Insert the text *Link to the NSPCC website.*

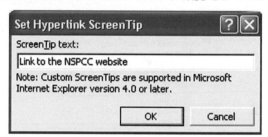

This text will be displayed when the mouse is rolled over the hyperlink in preview mode.

The text has become a hyperlink. When clicked this will link to the website for NSPCC.

9 Create a hyperlink for Save the Children, their URL (Uniform Resource Locator or web address) is *www.savethechildren.org.uk.*

10 Create a hyperlink for the World Wildlife Fund, their URL is *www.wwf.com.*
11 Save *Charities.htm.*
12 Preview the page in the browser.

John has decided to include the logos of all of the charities on the page. He wants to make each logo link to each charity's website.

Making a picture a hyperlink

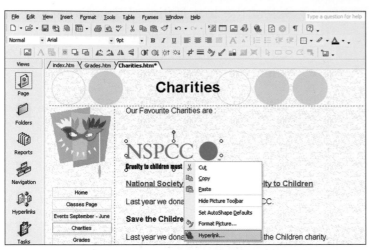

13 Open *charities.htm.*

14 Copy and paste the logo for the NSPCC into the charities page.

15 Use the picture toolbar to make the background of the logo transparent.

16 Position above the hyperlink *National Society for Prevention of Cruelty to Children.*

17 Right click on the logo and select *Hyperlink.*

18 Enter the address as shown.

19 Click on **Screen Tip**... and enter a suitable tip.

20 Open *website.doc* and copy in the logos for the other two charities, Save the Children and the World Wildlife Fund onto the web page.

21 Make the images hyperlinks to the charities' websites.

22 Insert the picture *Primary 1.jpg* into the Charities page.

The Charities page will look as follows.

3 Email systems

▶ **In this section you will learn about email.**
   Through examples you will gain skills which will assist in:
   - ■ Sending and receiving emails including address books.
   - ■ Use of attachments and carbon copying.

▶ **This is assessed through the following components:**
   - ■ Terminal examination(s).
   - ■ Assignment B1: Using the Internet.

Sending and receiving emails including address books

When you open your email account, the **Inbox** displays all emails that have been sent to you.

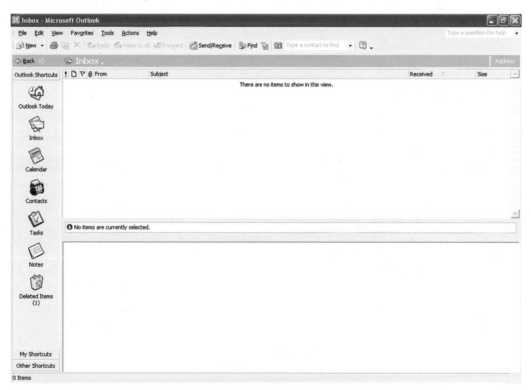

1 To send an email, click on the option **New**, and select *Mail Message*.

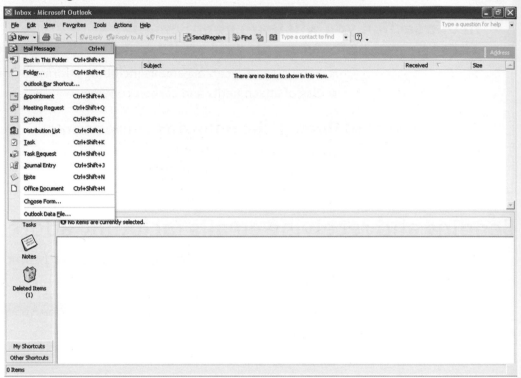

2 If the email address you are sending to is stored in your address book, then click on the icon **Address book**.

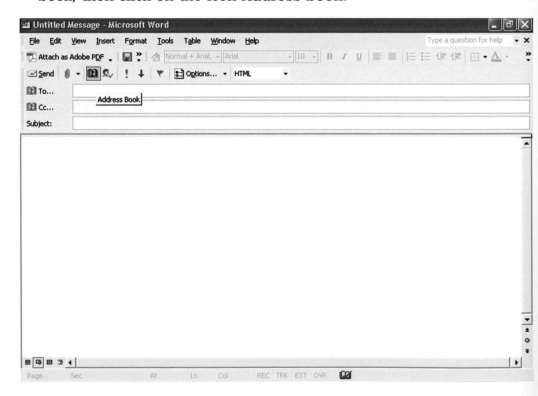

3 Then select the name from the stored list.

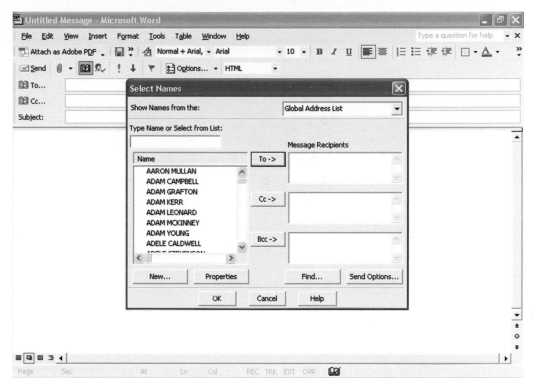

4 If the email address is not already stored, then click on the **New...** button to enter a new contact.

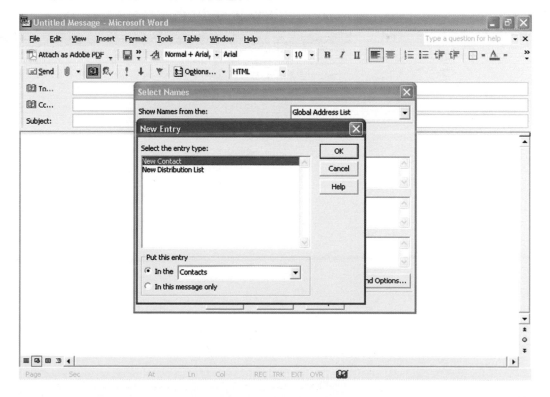

5 Complete the details in the form below. It is not important to complete all details, but make sure you enter the email address.

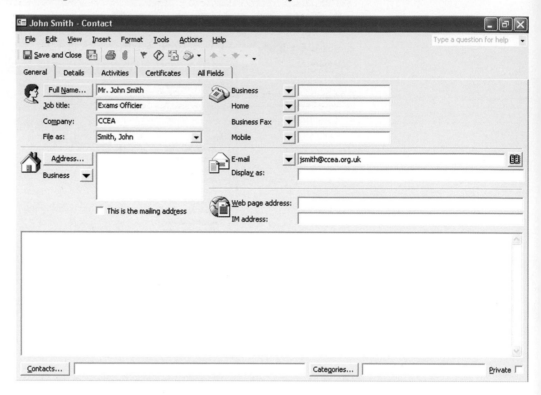

6 Then select **Save and Close** to return to the email. After entering subject details and the actual email, click on **Send**.

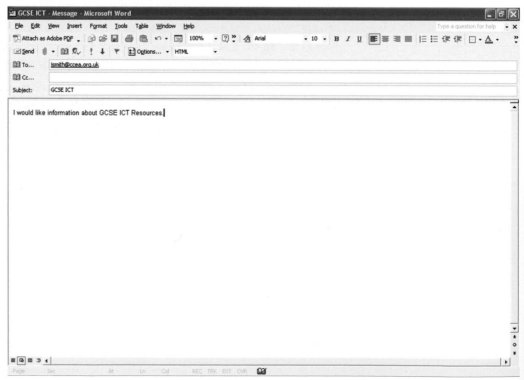

■ Use of attachments and carbon copying

If you wish to send the same email to another person it can be sent as a carbon copy (Cc).

1 Enter details in the subject box and create your email and press **Send**.

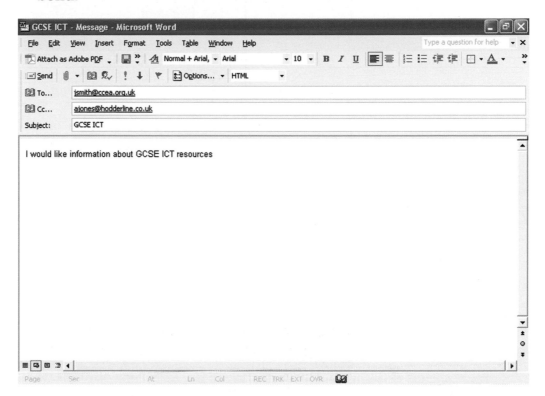

To send an attachment with an email, you would normally have the attachment, which could be a document or even a picture, stored in your **My Documents** folder. If you click on the icon for attaching files it will normally bring you to this folder. Then select your document and attach it by clicking **Insert** on the menu bar.

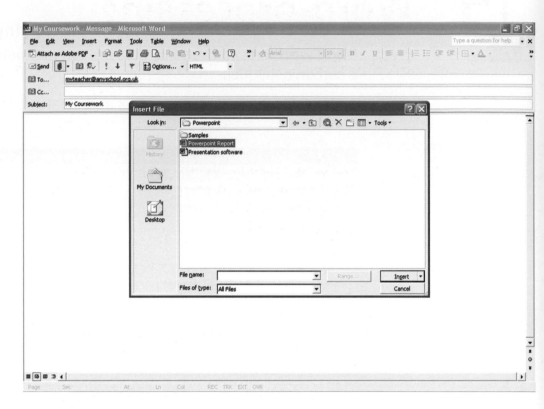

In the actual email you will see the document along with its type and size.

2 Then press **Send**.

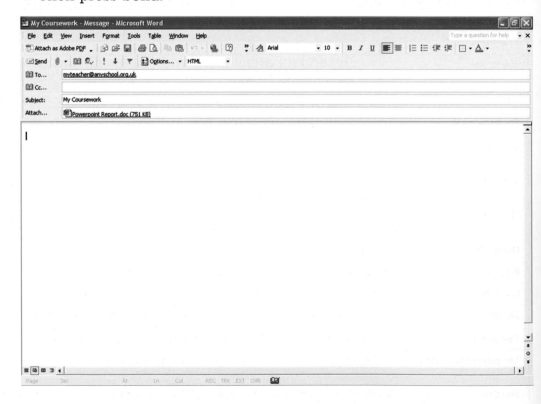

4 Word-processing packages C1(d)

▶ **In this section you will learn about word processing. Through examples you will gain skills which will assist in:**

- Moving, copying and deleting blocks of text.
- Formatting text, paragraphs and documents including the use of tables.
- Importing graphics.
- Use of templates.

▶ **This is assessed through the following components:**

- Terminal examination(s).
- Assignment A1: Design a multimedia presentation.
- Assignment A2: Produce a booklet or report.
- Assignment A3: Design a website.

Microsoft Word is an example of a word-processing package. All word-processing software packages have similar features. The table below illustrates some of these.

Feature	Detail
Bullet points	Allows the user to place and format bullet points to assist in presenting their document.
Drawing tools	Allows the user to add simple graphics to their documents such as arrows, predefined shapes and boxes.
File format	Allows the user to save documents in different formats such as RTF which can then be transferred to other word-processing or publishing packages.
Fonts	Allows the user to select a font type, size and style. Fonts can also be formatted into different colours.
Footer/header	Used to place titles, page numbers, dates etc. in your document.
Grammar checkers	More sophisticated word processors can check grammar, although they are limited due to the complex nature of the English language.
Import clip art/files	Places graphics in documents from other sources such as Clip Art, downloading from the Internet, transferring pictures from a digital camera and scanning graphics from hard copy sources.
Mail merge	Combines name and address details with a standard letter where the names and addresses are normally imported from a database. The end result is a set of personalised letters.
Online Help	Search using a keyword/topic for help. There are usually hypertext links to websites for detailed help.
Print preview	You can see the page before printed – WYSIWYG (What You See Is What You Get).
Spell checker	This is a built-in dictionary. The user can add their own words to the dictionary such as proper nouns.
Tables	Allows the user to place text/graphics into cells of a table. The user decides the number of rows and columns.
Text alignment	The user can select part or all of the text and align left, right, centre and justify.
Templates and wizards	The framework of document is provided for you, such as a business letter. Therefore the user does not need to worry about layout. They simply add text to predefined positions on the document.
Word count	This counts the number of words in a document. This is useful for an essay/coursework were there is a limit to the amount of words allowed.

Moving, copying and deleting blocks of text

This section is supported by the following digital media which may be accessed through www.hoddernorthern ireland.co.uk/ict/ Digestive System ReportA2- Word File.

When you have entered a block of text, it can be moved to another part of a document. It could also be replicated or even deleted.

Consider the text below. If we want to move the summary points to the beginning:

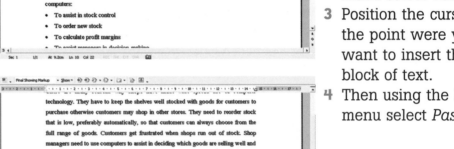

1 Using the cursor and the mouse, select the block of text. This text will automatically be highlighted.
2 Then using the **Edit** menu select *Cut*.
3 Position the cursor at the point were you want to insert the block of text.
4 Then using the **Edit** menu select *Paste*.

Formatting text, paragraphs and documents, including the use of tables

■ Font types, sizes and styles

1 You can choose a font type by selecting the **Format** menu.
2 Select **Font** ... .

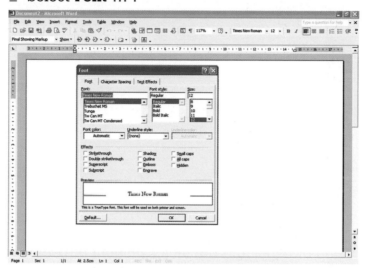

3 Then select your font, style and size.
4 Before returning to your document you can see what you selected in the **Preview** box.
5 To add special effects you can also click on a check box such as **Shadow**.
   To enhance the presentation of your document you may want to add colour. Normally the default colour is black.
6 To change the colour, select **Font color**.

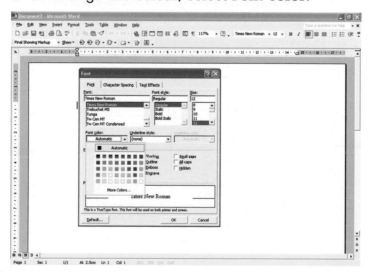

When selecting an appropriate colour, try using the option **More colors** ... .

■ Headers and footers

When producing booklets it would be a good idea to include page numbers and maybe the title of the document on each page.

1 From the **View** menu, select *Header and Footer*.

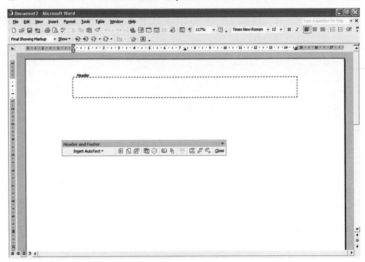

The buttons on the toolbar will allow you to toggle between the header (top of page) and the footer (bottom of page), select automatic page numbering, enter the current date and time.

2 Enter text into the box provided for either footer or header and then use the **Format menu** to select *font types, sizes and styles*.

3 Click **Close** on the Header and Footer toolbar to bring you back to your document.

■ Bullet points

1 To insert bullet points in your document, select **Format** menu and choose the option *Bullets and Numbering... .*

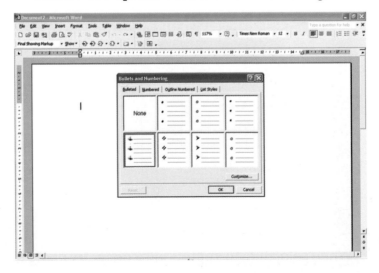

2 By clicking the **Customize...** button, you can select and format bullet points of your choice.

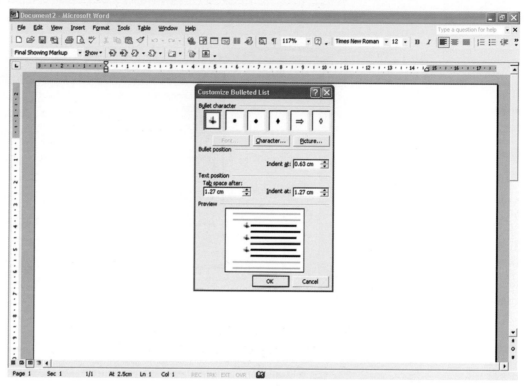

3 To use advanced bullet point techniques you can select **Insert** menu and the *Symbol...* option

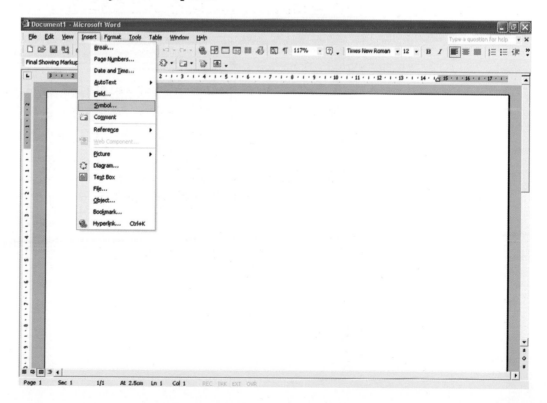

4 Then select the **Font** and choose Symbol font.

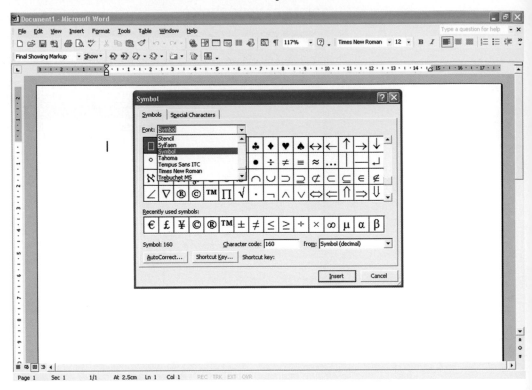

5 Then select a suitable symbol.

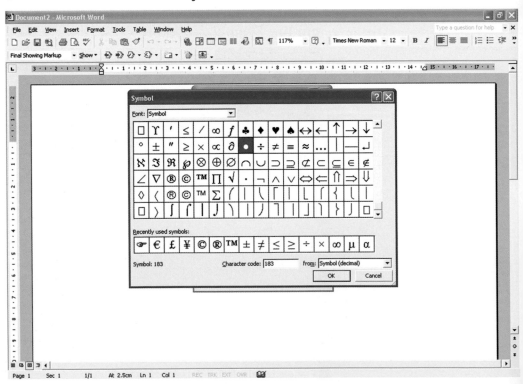

■ Formatting a paragraph

1 Select a paragraph, then select the **Format** menu and the *Paragraph...* option.

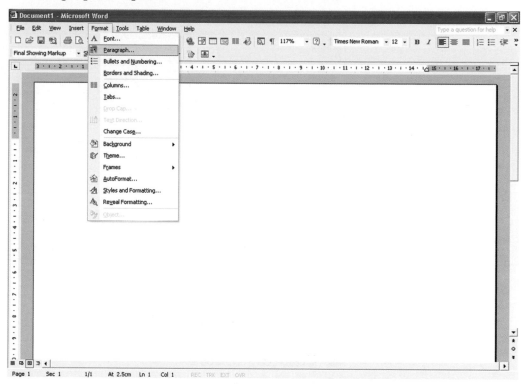

2 Select the **Line spacing** option to control the spacing in the paragraph selected.

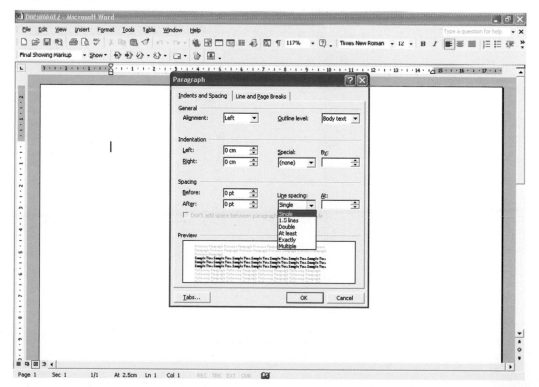

3 Select **Alignment** to choose *left*, *centered*, *right* or *justified*.

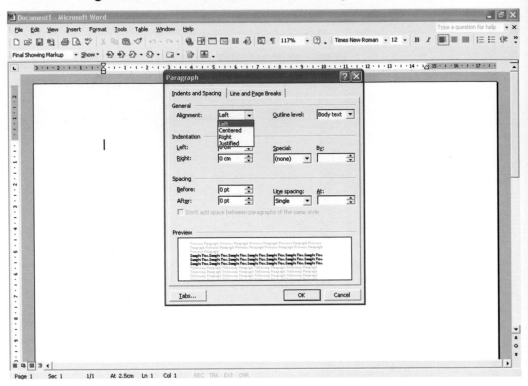

■ Creating tables

1 To insert a table, select **Table,** *Insert* and *Table... .*

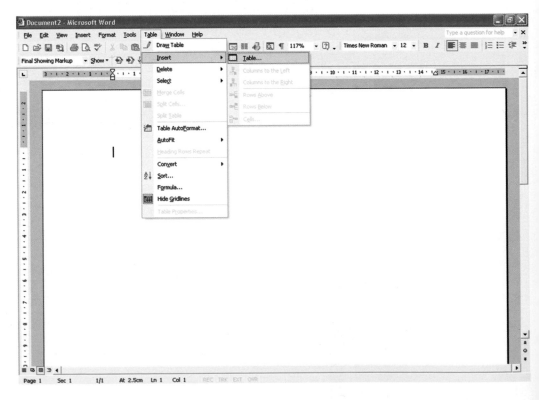

You will then be asked to specify the number of *columns* and *rows*.

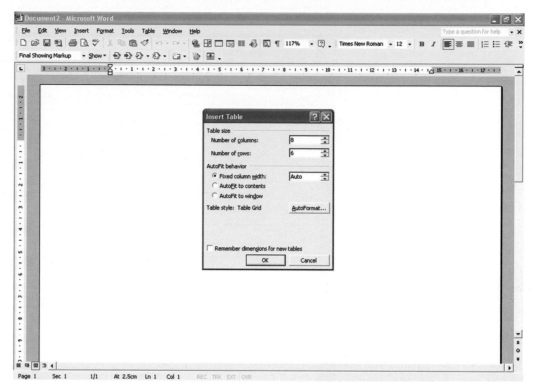

The table will normally appear with all cells similar in size.

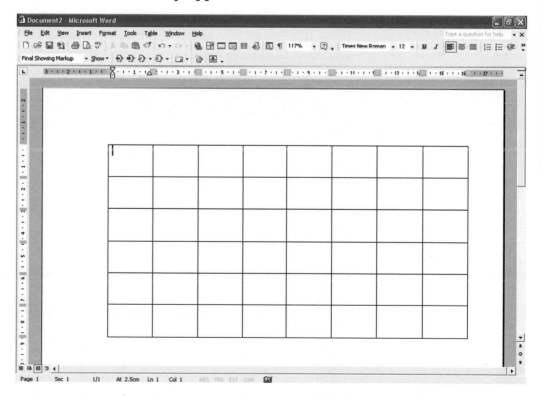

2 Select a group of cells and right click to select the option **Merge Cells**.

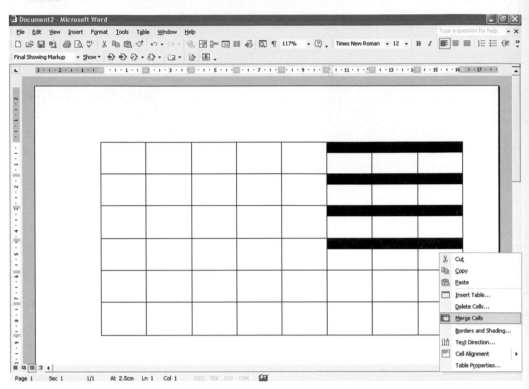

This allows the user to tailor their table to meet the requirements of their document.

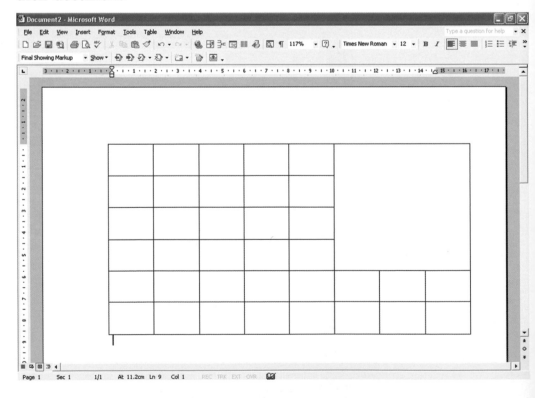

■ Spelling and grammar

■ To allow you to check spellings and grammar, select **Tools** and then *Spelling and Grammar…* .

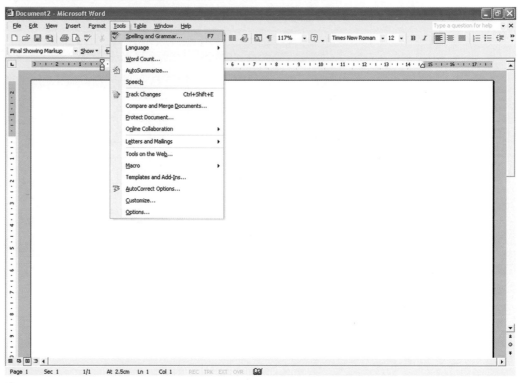

Importing graphics

1 Select the **Insert** menu, and then the *Picture* option.

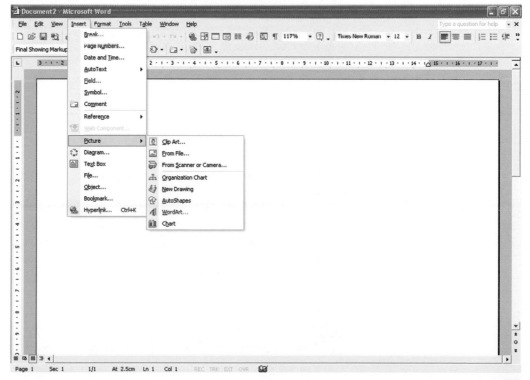

2 By selecting *WordArt...*, you are given a a choice of graphical type styles.

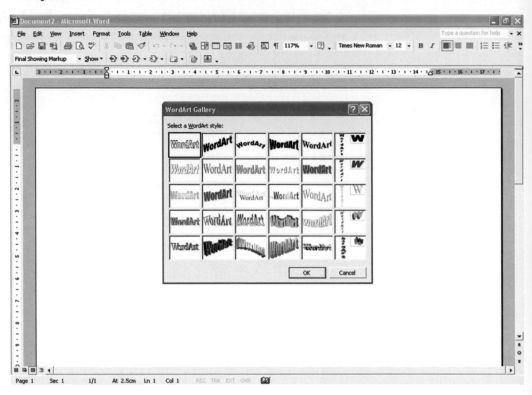

3 By selecting *Chart*, you can input values into a predefined table which are automatically used to create a chart.

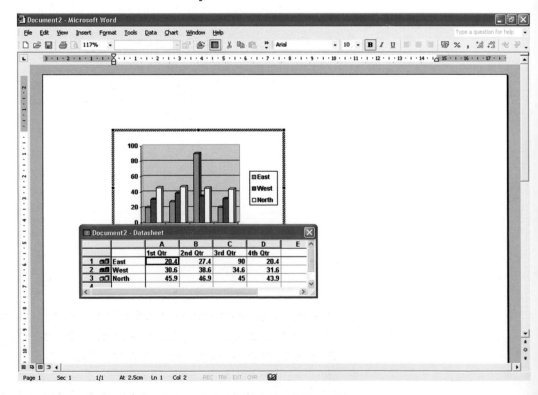

4 Select a chart and then right click on the menu that appears which allows further options such as **Chart Type**... .

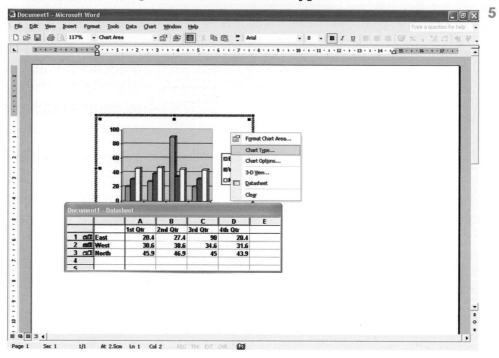

Click on the most suitable chart type.

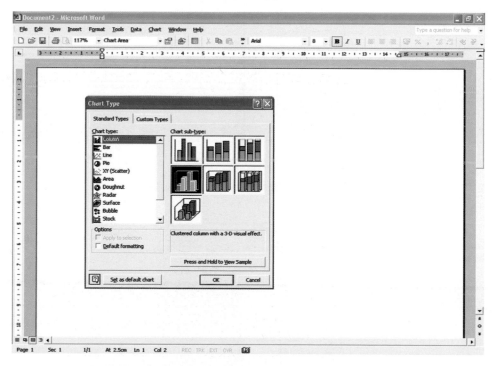

6 Use the **Insert** menu and select the option *Picture* and then *From File...* to import a graphic that was saved in My documents from a different source such as a digital camera.

7 Use the **Insert** menu and select the option *Picture* and then *Clip Art* to select a graphic from stored clip art or use a hypertext link to a relevant website to access more clip art images.

Use of templates

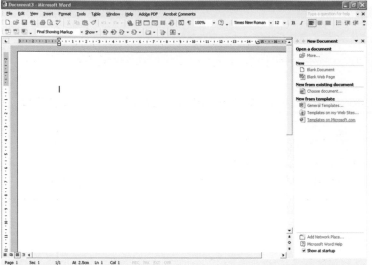

Using templates can assist the user with a particular layout. Within a word-processing package there are normally a number of predefined templates available to a user. With most software packages further templates can be found on a support website. To use a template, you need to:

1 Open the word-processing package.
2 On the right-hand side of the screen under **New from template,** select the option **General Templates**… .

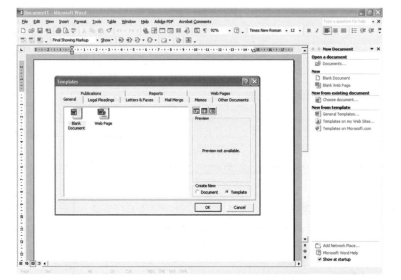

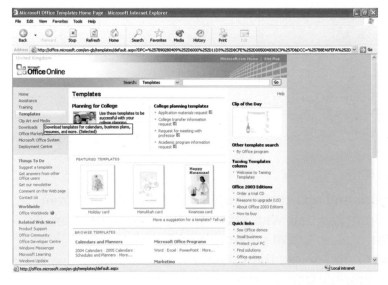

Advice on producing coursework assignment

■ Overall presentation

It is important to include:

- A front cover indicating clearly your Centre number and Candidate number.
- The title of the topic chosen and a relevant graphic illustrating your topic.
- You need to separate Activity 1 from Activity 2.
- Activity 1 is the actual report or booklet.
- Activity 2 is your report on how you produced your assignment.

■ Activity 1

This is the actual report or booklet, worth 14 marks.

I o gain the majority of these marks you must have evidence of:

- Graphs/charts from at least two sources.
- Font styles/ sizes.
- Bullet points.
- Creation and use of tables.
- Page numbering.
- Headers/footers.
- Justification.
- Indents and margins.
- Integration of text and graphics.
- Good overall appearance.

■ Activity 2

This is your report on how you produced the assignment and is worth 5 marks.

You should include the following as subtitles in this order:

- Topic chosen.
- Choice of ICT application.
- Features used.
- The information sources used.

Topic chosen

In this section you should make reference to the topic chosen in terms of the subject content and its place in your GCSE subject. You may wish to summarise the content chosen including text and graphics required.

Choice of ICT application

If you are using a word-processing package then refer to it. A good approach would be to explain the features of the package that you used in producing your booklet or report. This will help justify the choice of software package used.

■ The information sources used

In this section make reference to the information sources you used. For example, you may refer to websites or textbooks you used. Again screen dumps may help you explain these sources.

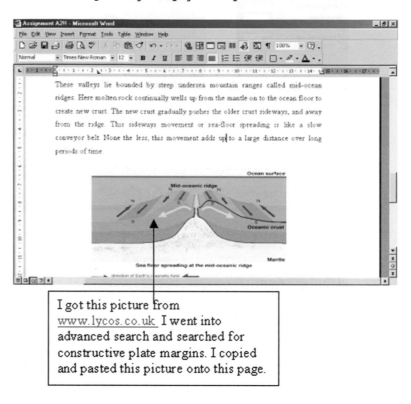

I got this picture from www.lycos.co.uk I went into advanced search and searched for constructive plate margins. I copied and pasted this picture onto this page.

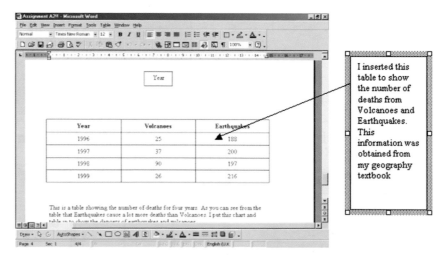

I inserted this table to show the number of deaths from Volcanoes and Earthquakes. This information was obtained from my geography textbook

5 Presentation packages C1(e)

> **In this section you will learn how to use a presentation package to effectively present information.**
> **Through the worked example you will gain skills which will assist in:**
> - formatting text.
> - inserting a combination of graphics, pictures, sound and video.
> - using buttons and timings to control the display sequence.
> - using any other special effects for display.
>
> **This is assessed through the following components:**
> - Terminal examination.
> - Assignment A1: Design a multimedia presentation.

The features of a presentation package

This section is supported by the following digital media which may be accessed through www.hoddernorthern ireland.co.uk/ict/.

Year8ICT.ppt
Year8IIMED.ppt

AssignmentA1.doc – An exemplar of assignment A1 is also provided with this section.

A presentation package provides users with the features to create presentations which combine text, graphics, sound and video. Users can select backgrounds for their presentation and can add buttons to allow users to navigate around it.

Users can create slide masters. A slide master is a slide which is used to include features which will appear on every slide. This slide is created only once and can be applied to all of the slides in the presentation.

Timings can also be added so that the presentation will play automatically without human intervention.

Consider the following scenario

As part of her GCSE English Language coursework Jane McIvor must give a ten minute talk to Year 8 pupils about the ICT facilities in her school. She has chosen to use a multimedia presentation to assist her in delivering the talk.

Jane will undertake the following tasks:

- Plan the content of the slides in her presentation.
- Design the layout of each slide.
- Design a master slide for the presentation.
- Collect the graphics, video and sounds required for the presentation.

Jane decides that there will be seven slides in the presentation. She then draws out the plan for navigating around her presentation.

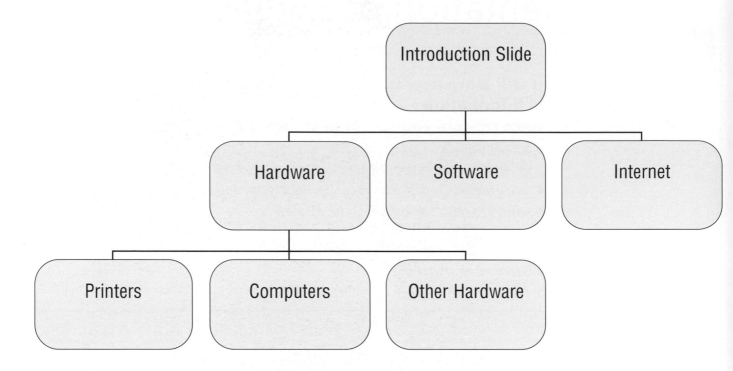

Having drawn the layout for the presentation, she uses a multimedia presentation tool, in this case Microsoft PowerPoint 2003.

How to create and edit a multimedia presentation

1 Open **PowerPoint**. You will see a blank slide.

2 Select *Slide Design* from the **Task** pane.
3 Select *Design Templates*.
4 Select *Cascade* as the design template.

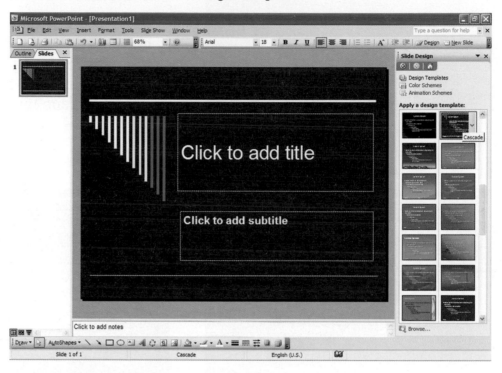

5 Click and add the title *Year 8 ICT*.
6 Add a subtitle *Facilities at our School*.
7 Save the presentation as *Year8ICT.ppt*

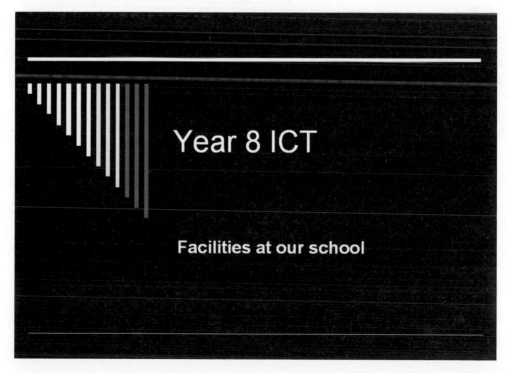

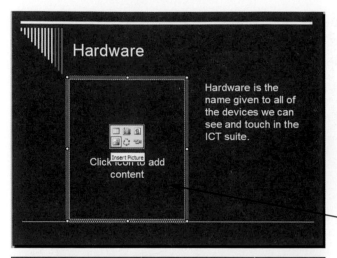

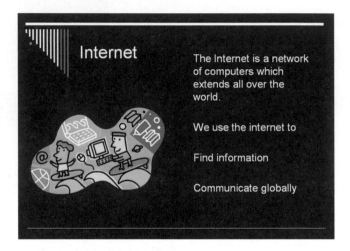

■ Adding new slides

The Hardware, Software and Internet Slides will contain a title, text and a graphic.

1 Select *Slide Layout* in the **Task** pane.
2 Insert three new slides which have title, text and content layout.
3 Insert the title, the text shown and a suitable picture into each slide.

Insert a picture by clicking on the insert picture icon, or the Clip

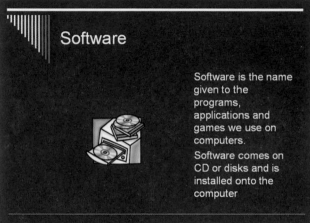

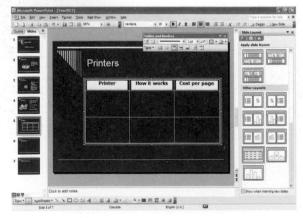

4 Save your presentation.

Jane wants to use a table in the Printers slide.

5 Add another slide which will contain a title and table.
6 Double click to add a table with 3 rows and 3 columns.

■ Formatting text in a multimedia presentation

1 Highlight the text in Row 1 as shown.
2 The text in Row 1 should be:
   ● Style: Bold
   ● Font: Verdana
   ● Font size: 16
   ● Aligned: Centre
3 Add text, graphics and colour as shown.

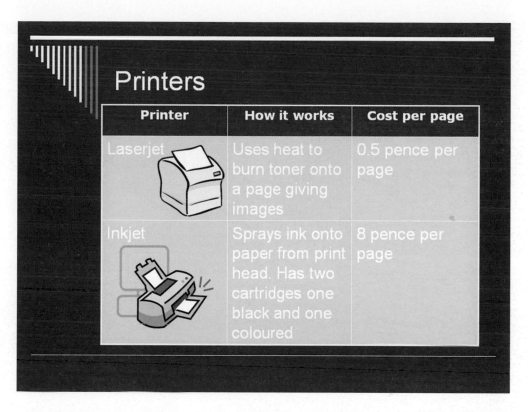

4 Insert the remaining slides with the text shown.
5 Select and insert your own graphics.

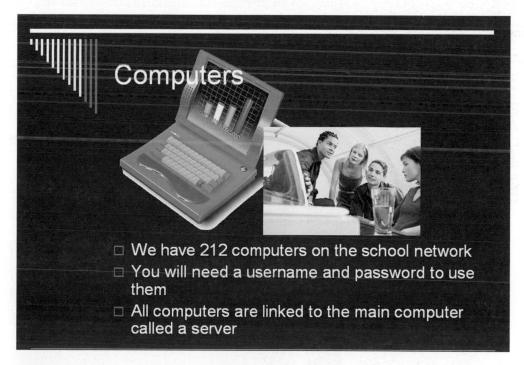

The basic slideshow has been created.
6 Save the presentation.
7 View the presentation.

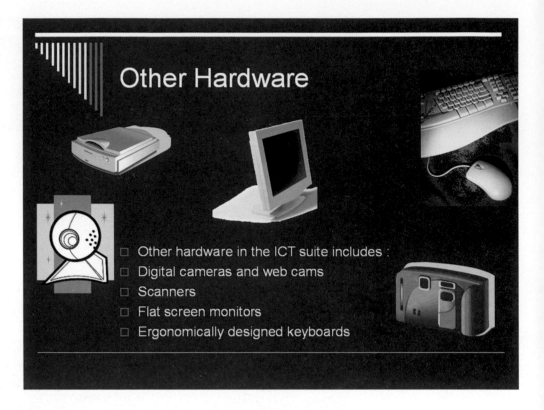

■ Inserting graphics behind text

Jane has improved the appearance of her first slide by including a graphic, placing it behind the text and changing the colour of the text.

1. Insert a graphic on the first slide.
2. Place the graphic behind the text.
3. Change the colour of the text and ensure the text is visible.

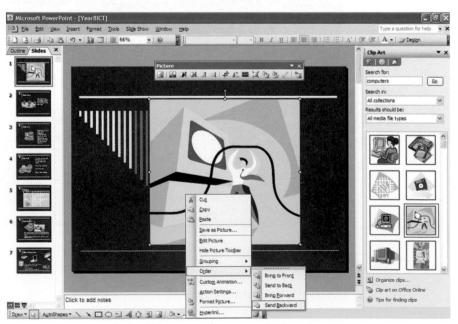

■ Using buttons to control the display sequence

Jane wants to link all of her slides together by using Action Buttons.

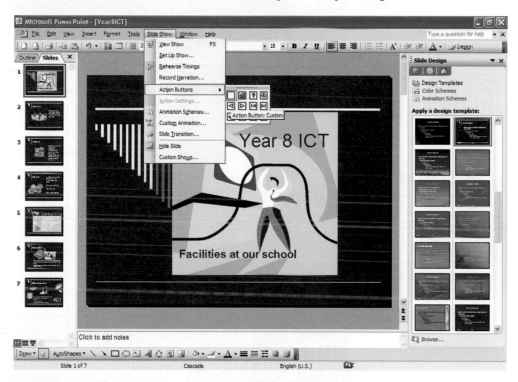

1 Select *Action Buttons* from the **Slide Show** menu.
2 Select *Action Buttons: Custom*.
3 Draw the outline of the button as shown.
4 In the *Action Settings* dialog box, link the button to **Slide 2 Hardware**.

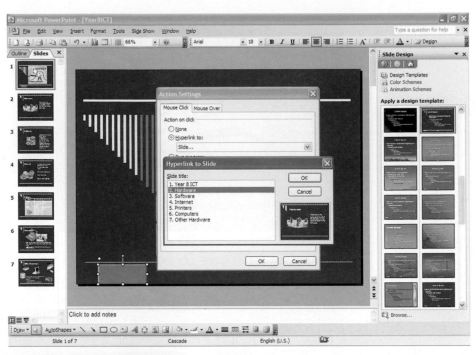

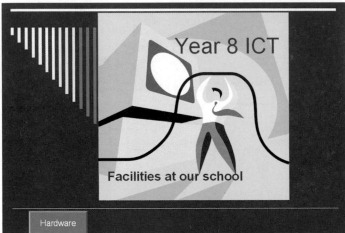

5 Using the textbox tool, add the word *Hardware* to the button.

6 Insert a button which links to the Software slide.

7 Add the word *Software* to the button, using the textbox tool.

8 Insert a button which links to the Internet slide.

9 Add the word *Internet* to the button, using the textbox tool.

10 Save your presentation.

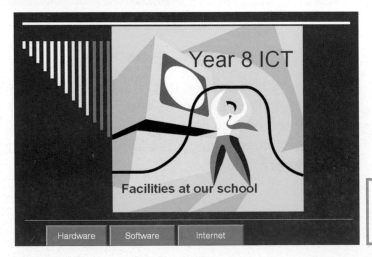

How can you return to the first slide in your presentation?

11 Test the navigation buttons.

▪ Creating a master slide

Jane wishes to add her name and the date to every slide. She also wants to add a button to each slide which will take the user back to slide 1. This could be done by adding the details to each slide individually. Another way of doing this is to create a slide master.

A slide master contains details which will appear on every slide in the presentation.

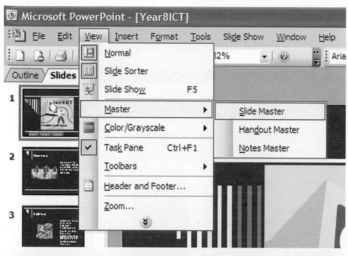

1 Create a slide master which will include Jane's name, the date and link back to slide 1.
2 Remove all of the boxes from the slide master so that it is blank.
3 Add an Action Button which will link to the first slide.
4 Add the text 'By Jane McIvor 12/12/04' to the top of the slide.
5 Close the Master slide view.
6 Press F5 to look at the slide show, each slide should now have the home button and Jane's name.
7 Add buttons which will link the hardware slide to the three slides about Printers, Computers and Other Hardware.
8 Save your presentation.

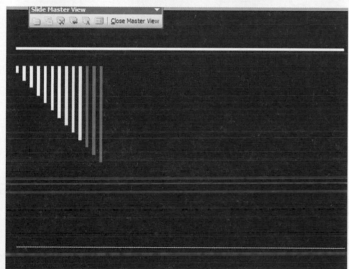

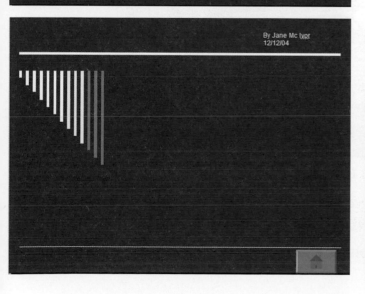

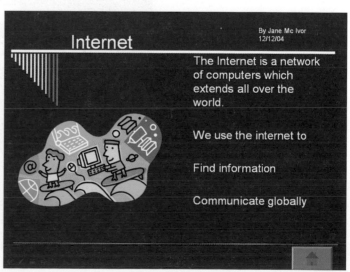

■ Inserting sound and video

Jane is going to include some sound effects to make her presentation more exciting for Year 8.

PowerPoint allows sound to be added from a file, clipart or from a CD.

1 Insert a suitable sound as shown to introduce the presentation.

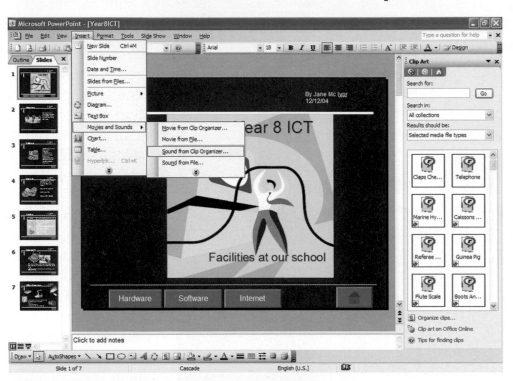

2 Click Automatically, this means that the sound will play when the presentation is run.

This icon indicates that a sound has been added:

3 Run the presentation and listen to the sound.

■ Using special effects for display

1 Select *Slide Transition* in the **Task** pane.
2 Click on the thumbnail of Slide 2 in the **Slide** pane.
3 Select *Cover Left* from the **Task** pane.
4 Select a *Medium* speed for the slide transition.
5 Apply 3 slide transitions to three slides.
6 View the slide show.
7 Save the presentation.

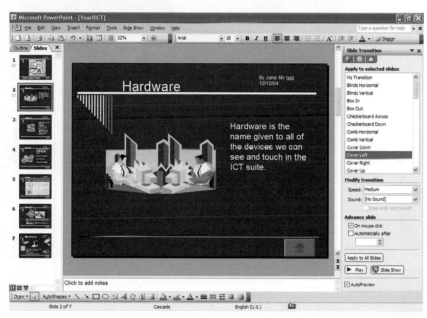

Extension activities

■ Using timings to control the display sequence

Jane has decided to make a new copy of the slide show to run in the school foyer.

1 Save your presentation as *timedyear8.ppt*.
2 Go to the Master Slide and remove the Home button.
3 Close the Slide Master view.
4 Click on the thumbnail of Slide 1 and remove all of the buttons from the slide.
5 Click on *Slide Transition* in the **Task** pane.
6 Uncheck the button which says *On mouse click*.
7 In the *Advance Slide* section tick the box which says *Automatically after*.
8 Set the seconds to 3.
9 Click on Apply to All Slides.
10 Save your presentation.
11 View the presentation.

■ Printing slides

1 Select File.

2 Select Print Preview.

3 Select Handouts (3 slides per page).

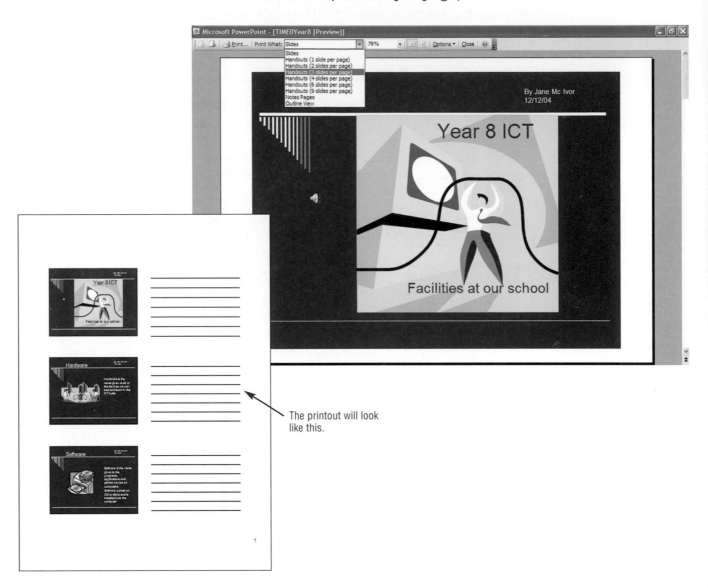

The printout will look like this.

6 Graphics packages C1(f)

> **In this section you will learn about graphics.**
> **Through examples you will gain skills which will assist in:**
>
> - Creating and manipulating images.
>
> **This is assessed through the following components:**
>
> - Terminal examination(s).
> - Assignment B1: Using the Internet.

Adobe Photoshop is an example of a graphics package. All graphics software packages have similar features. The table below illustrates some common features of graphics packages.

Feature	Detail
Draw lines	Lines can be straight or curved. They can be freehand.
Pre-defined shapes	Shapes such as rectangles and circles can be drawn.
Size	Change the size of the shape. Referred to as scaling.
Cropping	Cut out part of an image.
Stretch	Shape can be stretched horizontally or vertically.
Rotate/flip	Shape can be rotated through an angle either clockwise or anticlockwise. A shape can be reflected through an angle.
Colour	A paint palette can be used. Change the colour of lines. Change the colour of objects.
Fill	Areas with shading or patterns.
Zoom	Allows an area of the screen to be seen more closely.
Clip art	An inbuilt library of drawings.
Tool palette	Uses icons to show tools available such as a brush or a magnifying tool.
Text boxes	Text can be added to a graphic.
Save	Graphics can be saved in different formats.

Creation and manipulation of images

Graphics can be inserted into a word-processed document. To do this select the menu **Insert** and then the option **Picture.** You will then be given a choice of a number of external sources where a graphic can be imported from. Using Clip Art is the easiest choice as it does not require another device, such as a digital camera, to be attached. Using the web links within Clip Art will give you more choice.

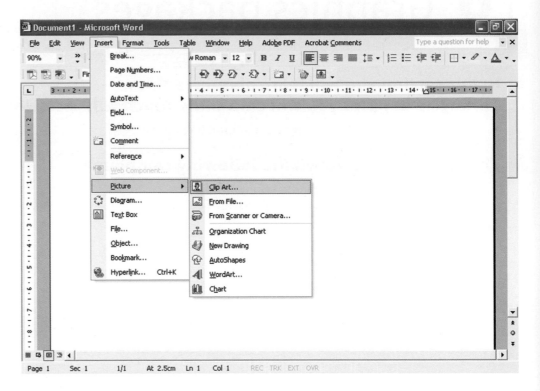

1 Select the **Insert** menu and the option **Picture**.
2 Click on **Clip Art**. . . .
3 On the right-side of the screen click on **Clips Online**.

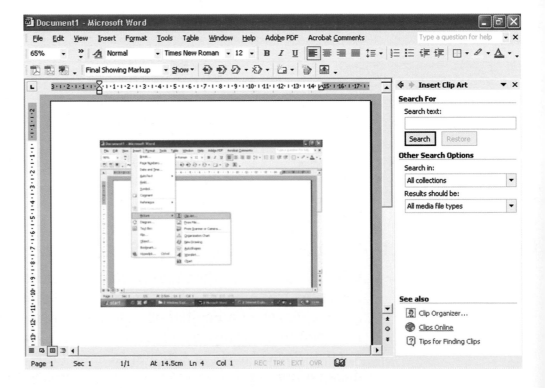

This will link to Microsoft's website (make sure you have an Internet connection for this to happen) where you can choose a relevant category.

4 In this example select **Technology**.

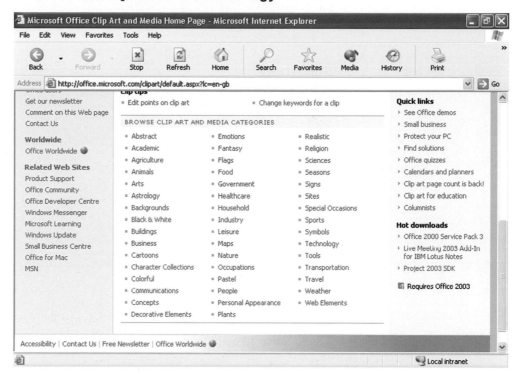

This will then display thumbnails illustrating the clip art. Once you decide on the required image, clicking it will display a shortcut menu.

5 Select **Copy** to place the image into the **Selection Basket**.

6 Click **Download item** to place the clip art into the *Collection List*.

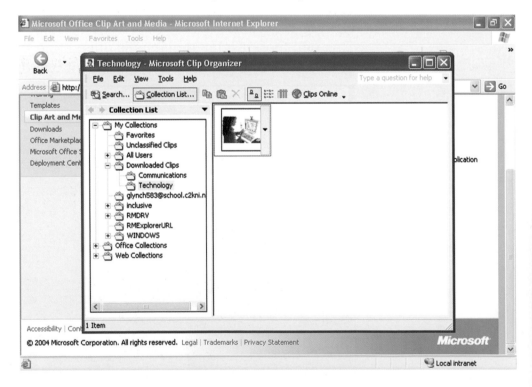

7 To manipulate the image, click on the arrow and select **Open Clip In**. . . .

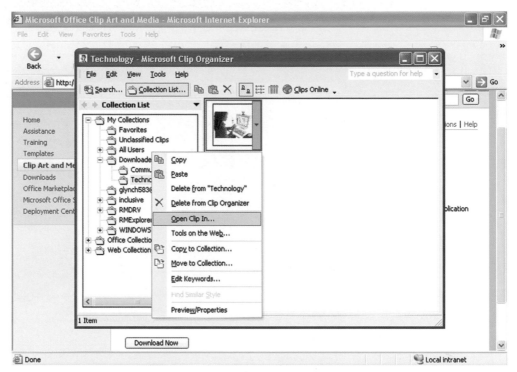

The image will appear in a graphics package in JPEG format ready for manipulation.

8 Select the menu **Image** and the option *Crop* to control what the image will look like.

The picture is rectangular at present.

9 Click the oval radio button to change the shape of the image.

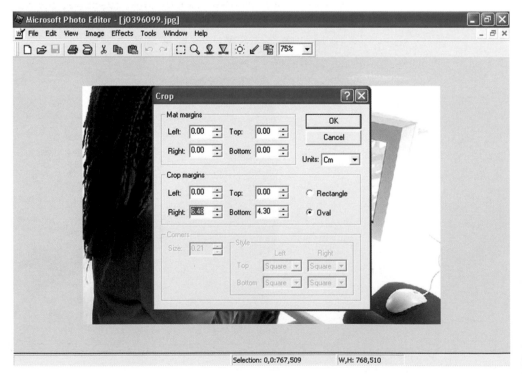

10 Select the menu **Image** and the option *Resize* to control the size of the image. Changing it to 50% in width and height will reduce the image to a quarter of its size.

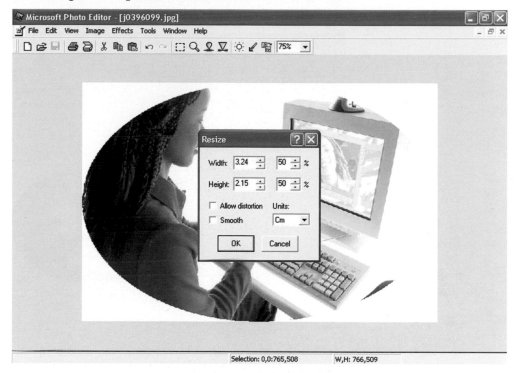

The image is now a quarter of its original size.

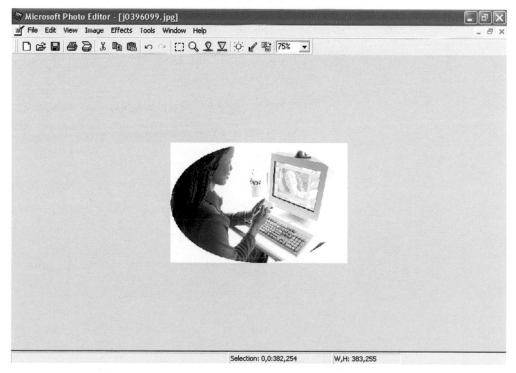

11 Select the menu **Image** and the option *Rotate* to control the image orientation.

12 Clicking on the **Mirror** radio button can change the position of the lady to the right side from the left side.

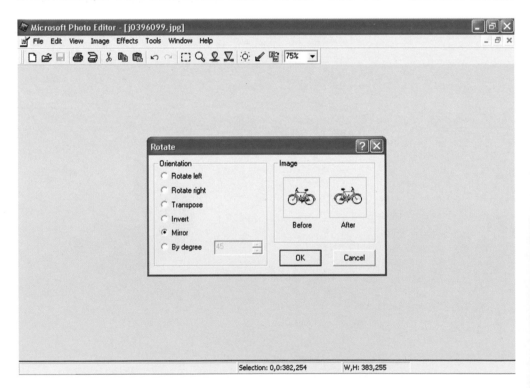

Once you have finished manipulating the graphic it can be saved as a jpeg file to a relevant folder such as **My Pictures.**

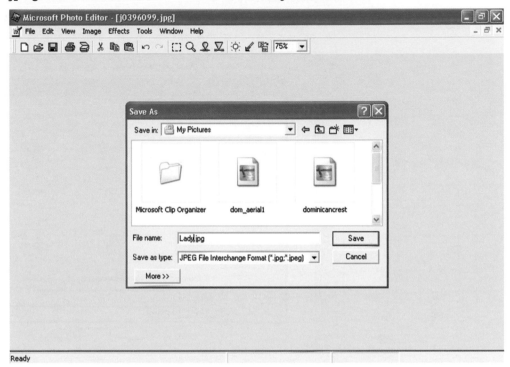

13 To place the picture in a word-processed document, select the menu **Insert** and the option *Picture* and *From File....*

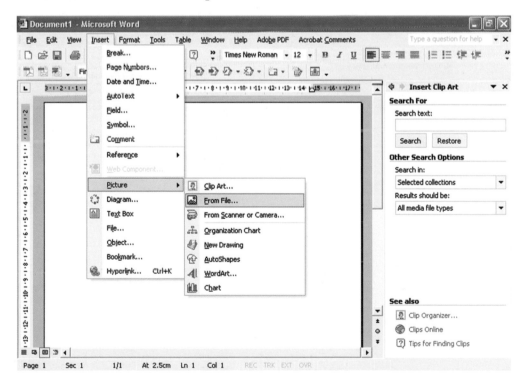

14 Select your pictures folder and click on the relevant picture and click on **Insert**.

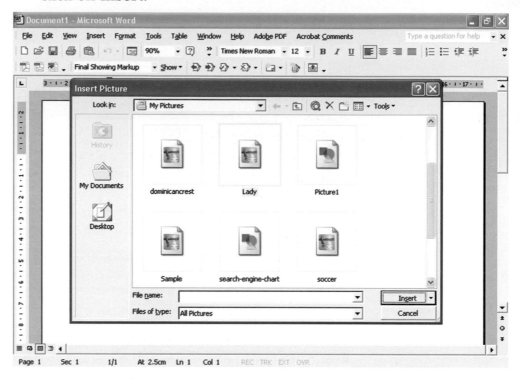

The picture will appear in your document along with your **Picture toolbox** for further editing if the need arises.

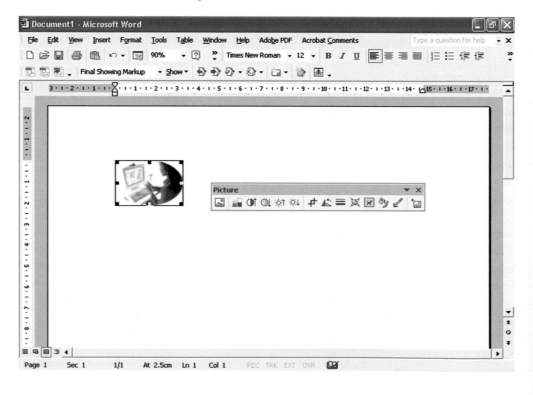

7 Information handling packages c1(g)

> **In this section you will learn about information handling. Through the worked example you will gain skills which will assist in:**
>
> - creating and editing a database.
> - amending the structure of a database.
> - validating data.
> - simple searching and sorting.
> - complex searching on two or more criteria which may include the use of logical operators.
> - formatting reports.
> - importing data, in a variety of forms, from an electronic source.
> - mail-merging.
>
> **This is assessed through the following components:**
>
> - Terminal Examination.
> - Assignment A2: Produce a booklet or report.
> - Assignment A3: Design a website.
> - *Assignment B2: Databases. This assignment is compulsory for all students who study the short or full GCSE course.*

The features of a database package

This section is supported by the following digital media which may be accessed through www.hoddernorthern ireland.co.uk/ict/.
Music.mdb – a Microsoft Access database file
Accompanist.xls – a Microsoft Excel file
Mainletter.doc – a Microsoft Word file
Mergedletter.doc – a Microsoft Word file
AssignmentB2.doc – An example of assignment B2 designed for submission to CCEA.

A database package is designed to allow users to collect and structure data. Data is structured into records. Each record is made up of a field and each field has a data type. There are a number of records in a single table.

The database package will provide:

- Query facility – which allows the user to quickly find information which fulfil given criteria.
- Forms – the user can create forms to capture data on screen.
- Method of validating data, for example, range checks and presence checks can be taken when data is being entered to ensure it is correct.
- Reports – reports can be generated using the data or query results. These reports can be grouped in particular fields.
- Relationships – tables can be linked together using relationships. This cuts down on the amount of data which has to be stored and makes the searching and sorting of data more efficient.

How to create and edit a database

In Section C2 you will study the features of a relational database. As part of your coursework, Assignment B2, you are required to use a database to produce information.

Consider the following scenario

The Earhart School of Music is run by Ruth Earhart. She offers pupils the chance to study three musical instruments at three different grades. Any pupil can study violin, piano or flute to grades 3, 4 or 5. Some pupils study more than one instrument. Ruth wants to keep a record of her pupils and their details. She also wants to record information about when they pay to take the music examinations.

Pupils currently fill out a manual form like the one in the picture below:

Earhart School of Music

Name:

Address:

Town:

Postcode:

Do you need an accompanist for your exam?   Y/N

Parent signature:

Date:

Having studied database software at a night class she has decided to set up a database with the following structure. Here is a typical record from the database.

PupilNumber	Surname	Forename	Street	Town	Postcode	AccompanistRequired	DateJoined
1000	Black	Ellen	23 Long Road	Coleraine	BT99 0JJ	Yes	12-Dec-03

Creating a database

There are many different types of database software. Microsoft Access is a database software tool. In order to create a database:

1 Click on **File** and select *New.*
2 Click on *Blank database.*

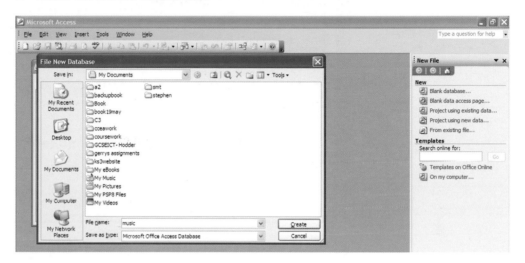

3 Give the file the name *Music.*
4 Click *Create.*
5 Select the Tables tab.
6 Double click on *Create table in Design View.*

The *Table Design* window will appear.

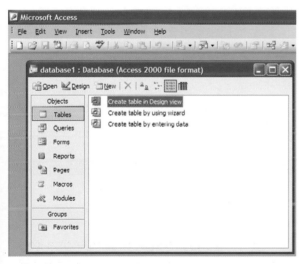

■ How to structure a database

You can read about fields and records and data types in Section C2 of this book.

Data in a database is organised into fields.

1 Enter the following field names into the Table Design window.

2 Save the Table as *Pupil.*

The Table Design window will look like the one shown on the left when all of the fields have been entered and the table has been saved.

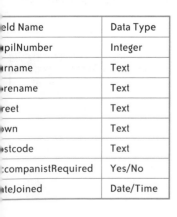

eld Name	Data Type
pilNumber	Integer
rname	Text
rename	Text
reet	Text
wn	Text
stcode	Text
ccompanistRequired	Yes/No
teJoined	Date/Time

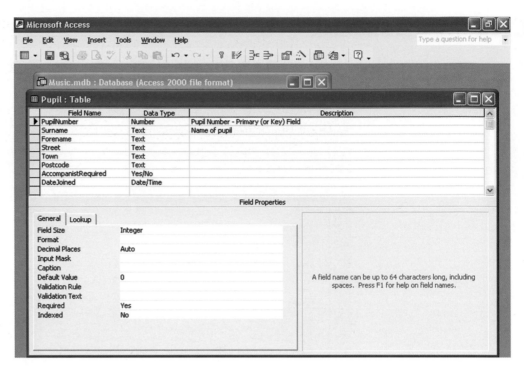

■ Selecting a key field for the table

In Section C2 you can read about the purpose of a Key Field or Primary Key.

> In this case the field PupilNumber will be the Key Field.

What is a Key Field and why do we need one?

To set PupilNumber as the Key Field:

1 Highlight the row which contains the field PupilNumber.
2 Click on the Primary Key icon.

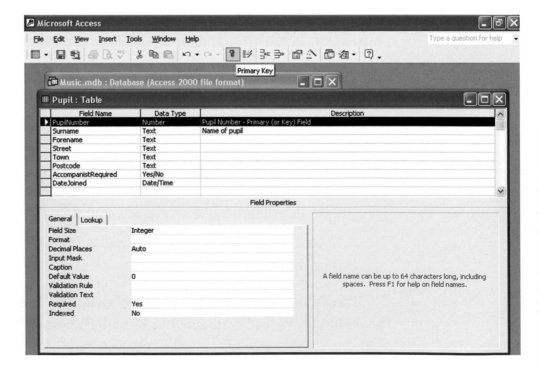

A key symbol will appear beside the PupilNumber field showing that it is now the Primary Key or Key Field in the Pupil table.

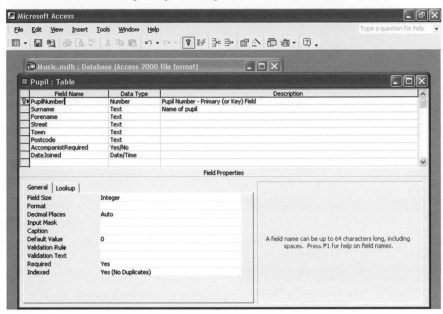

Validation and input masks

Once the table structure has been set up data can be entered into the table. In Section C2 you will study the way in which data can be validated when it is being input to a computer system.

When data is being collected it should be validated to ensure that it is in the correct range or is of the correct type. Microsoft Access has some special facilitates which allow for validation and format checking.

■ Input masks

An input mask controls how data is entered into the database. The input mask defines the format of the data being entered. Here are some examples:

0   Accepts a digit 0 to 9. Plus and minus signs not allowed. Entry required.

9   Accepts a digit (0 to 9) or SPACE. Plus and minus signs not allowed. Entry NOT required.

\#   Accepts a digit or space. Plus and minus signs allowed. Entry NOT required.

L   Accepts a letter A to Z. Entry required.

?   Accepts a letter A through Z. Entry NOT required.

A   Accepts a letter or digit. Entry NOT required.

a   Accepts a letter or digit. Entry NOT required.

&   Any character or a space. Entry required.

C   Any character or a space. Entry NOT required.

<   Will convert all characters that follow to lowercase.

>   Will convert all characters that follow to uppercase.

Examples of useful input masks:

Sample input mask	Acceptable values
(000) 00-00000	(028) 71-77775
(0000) AAA-AAAAA	(9445) 555-PUPIL
#999	−20 or 123
>L????L?000L0	BLACKGR678H4 YYY R 765Y8
>L<?????????????	Annabel
>LL00000-0000	AC45654-3209

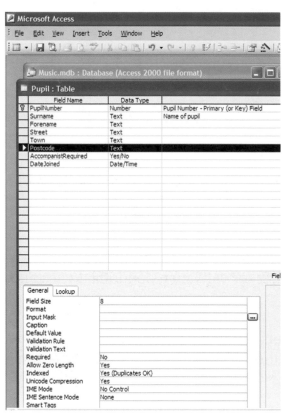

There are some ready–made input masks available in Microsoft Access. One of these is for a postcode. This can be applied to the postcode field by following the steps outlined.

1. Select the **Postcode** field.
2. Click on the **Input Mask** row.
3. Click on the ellipsis icon [...].
4. Select the Postal Code Input Mask from the Input Mask Wizard.

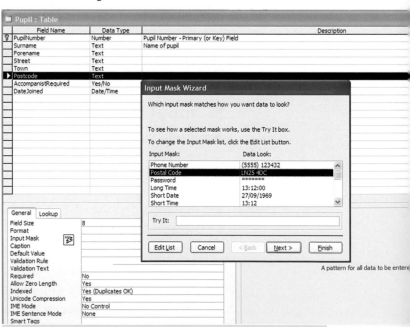

In order to ensure that the space in the Postcode appears we select the *With the symbols in the mask* option button.

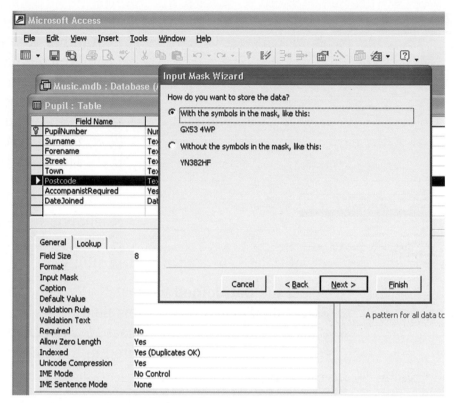

The Input Mask for the postcode now appears in the Input Mask row.

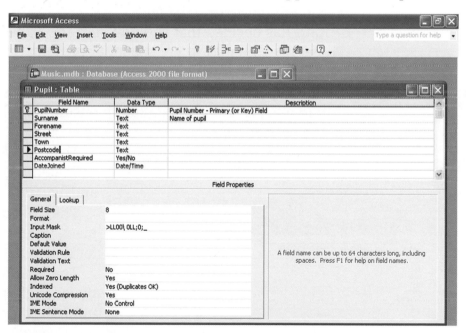

Design input masks for each of the following:

- Ensure that the PupilNumber field accepts four digits between 0 and 9. Entry is required.
- Ensure that the Surname and Forename fields format data with capital letters at the beginning of each field.

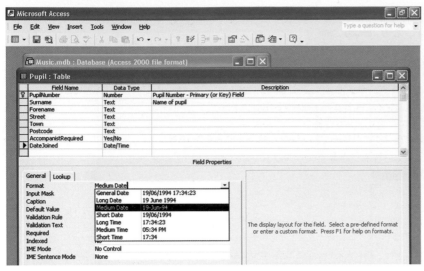

Formatting the Date Joined field

Another way of controlling the way in which data is to be held in a database is to use some of the data formatting tools.

Ruth wants DateJoined to be held in the following format: 24-Apr-04.

The field can be formatted so that regardless of how the data is entered into the database, it will be shown in the required format. This is done by using the Format utility.

1 Select the **DateJoined** field.
2 Select the **Format** row for this field.
3 Click on the **List** box and select *Medium Date.* This will ensure that the date joined data is captured in the correct format.

■ Validation in Microsoft Access

Validation ensures that data is present, in the correct range and format. Section C2 covers validation.

Ruth has decided that she will start the PupilNumber field at 1000. There are 25 pupils in her school at present. She has decided that the school will never have more than 100 pupils.

The PupilNumber field will have values 1000–1100.

She wishes to add validation to ensure that the PupilNumber data is in the correct range.

Microsoft Access allows data to be validated using the *Validation Rule* and *Validation Text* rows.

The *Validation Rule* row is the place where the range check or rule for data entry is placed.

The *Validation Text* is the text which will appear in a message box if the data entered does not satisfy the *Validation Rule*.

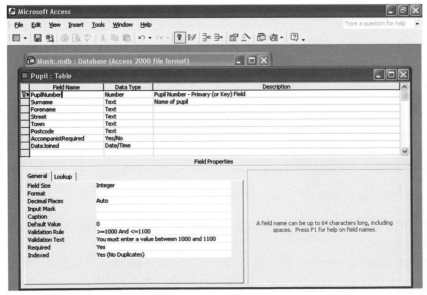

> You will test the validation in the table later.

1 In the *Validation Rule* row enter: >=1000 and <=1100.
2 In the *Validation Text* row enter: You must enter a value between 1000 and 1100.

Ruth wishes to make sure that the DateJoined data is validated. The school has been opened since September 2003.

3 Create a Validation Rule for the DateJoined field.
4 Save and Close the table Pupil.

Creating a data entry form

Section C2 examines the role of data capture forms in data entry.

Database software usually provides some method of designing forms for data capture. Access allows users to create such forms. It makes data entry more user friendly.

1 Select the **Forms** tab.
2 Select *Create form by using wizard*.

The *Form Wizard* window will appear.

3 Select the table **Pupil** from the Tables/Queries drop-down list.
4 Move all of the Available Fields into the Selected Fields box by clicking >>.
5 Click Next.

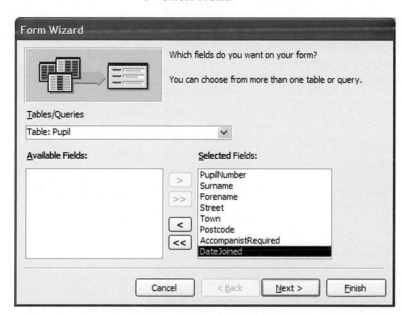

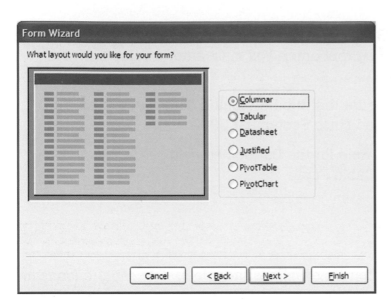

6 Select Columnar layout.

7 Click Next.

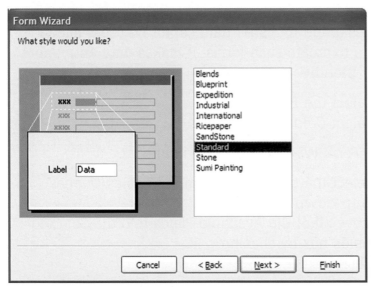

8 Select Standard style for the form layout.

9 Click Next.

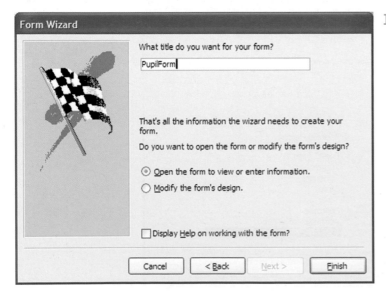

10 Save the form as PupilForm.

The finished form is shown on the left. The form can be used to view data or to enter new data.

11 To enter new data click on the new record icon. ▶✱
12 Using the newly designed form, enter the following data into the database.

PupilNumber	Surname	Forename	Street	Town	Postcode	AccompanistRequired	DateJoined
1000	Black	Ellen	23 Long Road	Coleraine	BT99 0JJ	Yes	12-Dec-03
1001	Green	Hugh	27 High Street	Portstewart	BT96 1UJ	Yes	21-Oct-04
1002	Matson	Mary	1 Shipquay Street	Coleraine	BT99 9YY	No	19-Sep-04
1003	Ross	Richard	23 Main Street	Coleraine	BT99 2WW	Yes	12-Jun-04
1004	Barkley	Susan	12 Culmore Ave	Portrush	BT95 5TT	Yes	21-Oct-04
1005	Mackle	Edward	120 West Road	Portstewart	BT96 1IK	No	12-Jun-04
1006	Smith	Rochelle	5 The Strand	Coleraine	BT99 2WG	Yes	21-Sep-04
1007	Kane	Philip	98 Richmond Park	Portrush	BT95 5XD	Yes	21-Oct-04
1008	Rawdon	Kim	12 Clarendon Park	Portstewart	BT96 1UJ	Yes	18-Aug-04
1009	Parke	Anne	78 William Street	Coleraine	BT99 2SR	Yes	21-Oct-04
1010	Rodgers	Caroline	1 Orchid Square	Portstewart	BT96 1OH	Yes	14-Aug-04
1011	Garner	Heather	4 Atlantic Road	Coleraine	BT99 2WW	Yes	21-Oct-04
1012	Caldwell	Rose	90 Portlock Ave	Coleraine	BT99 3GH	Yes	12-Jun-04
1013	Buckley	Brenda	73 Papworth Drive	Portrush	BT95 5HG	Yes	21-Oct-04
1014	Anderson	Claire	99 Drummond Park	Portstewart	BT96 1QQ	No	19-Sep-04
1015	Thompson	June	19 Bishop Street	Coleraine	BT99 7YII	Yes	01-Sep-04
1016	Kelly	Charles	14 Main Street	Portstewart	BT96 1EW	No	12-Jun-04
1017	Lambe	Laura	51 Lower Pier	Portrush	BT95 6YH	Yes	07-Sep-04
1018	Huey	Earl	77 Woodbrook West	Coleraine	BT99 9UH	No	21-Oct-04
1019	Walsh	John	19 Epworth Park	Coleraine	BT99 3JK	Yes	21-Oct-04
1020	Evans	Orla	23 Wesley Street	Portrush	BT95 6TF	Yes	21-Oct-04
1021	Smyth	Naomi	88 Lisdillon Road	Portstewart	BT96 1VS	Yes	12-Jun-04
1022	Walker	Michael	91 Hillview Park	Coleraine	BT99 1QS	No	14-Sep-04
1023	Paynter	Mirella	85 Foyle Road	Coleraine	BT99 5DC	No	12-Jun-04
1024	Swann	Margaret	13 Petri Way	Portrush	BT95 6UK	Yes	21-Oct-04
1025	Cunningham	John	107 Baronscourt	Portstewart	BT96 1NB	Yes	27-Oct-04
1026	Sheridan	Moorlene	100 Garden City	Coleraine	BT99 4BN	Yes	08-Nov-04
1027	McNicholl	David	1 Talbot Ave	Portrush	BT95 5TR	Yes	12-Jun-04
1028	Lynch	Ivor	14 Hamstead Park	Portstewart	BT96 1AF	No	12-May-04
1029	Doherty	Jack	16 Greenpark Close	Coleraine	BT99 7HH	Yes	05-May-04
1030	Moore	Amanda	8 Kensington Drive	Portrush	BT95 5TD	Yes	12-Jun-04

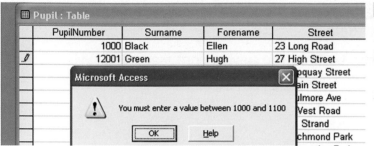

Test the validation

1 Open the Pupil table in table view.
2 Go to the second record in the Pupil table.
3 Change the PupilNumber to 12001. You will see that validation text appears, click OK.
4 Return the PupilNumber to 1001.

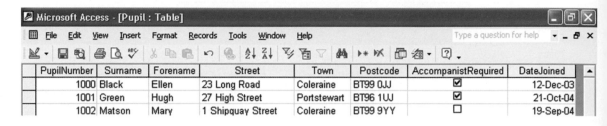

5 Now test your validation for DateJoined data.

Ruth has now decided to record information about when pupils pay for their examinations.

She needs to know:

- Which pupil has paid.
- What the pupil has paid for .
- The date of the payment.
- The amount of the payment.

One pupil studies many instruments. She proposes a table of the following structure.

Field Name	Data Type
ReceiptNumber	AutoNumber
PupilNumber	Number
GradeTaken	Text
Instrument	Text
DateOfPayment	Date/Time
Amount	Currency

1 Create this table in the table design window.
2 Make ReceiptNumber the Primary Key.
3 Save the table as *PupilReceipt*.

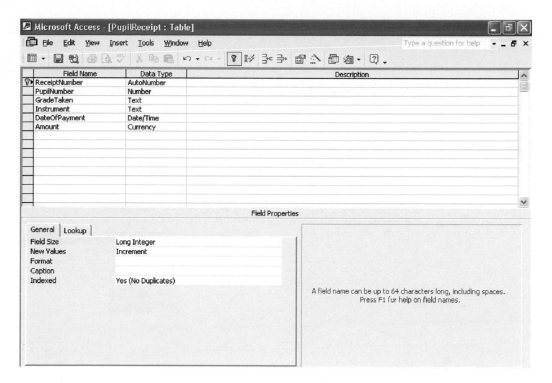

4 Add suitable validation to the database to take account of the following:

■ The GradeTaken data can only be "Grade 4", "Grade 5" or "Grade 6".
■ The instruments taken at the school are "Violin", "Piano" or "Flute".
■ The amount for each grade taken is between £20 and £60.

■ Relationships

The Microsoft Access database now has two tables. It is possible to link these two tables so that data can be accessed from both of them at once. You can look at the advantages of string data in a relational database in Section C2.

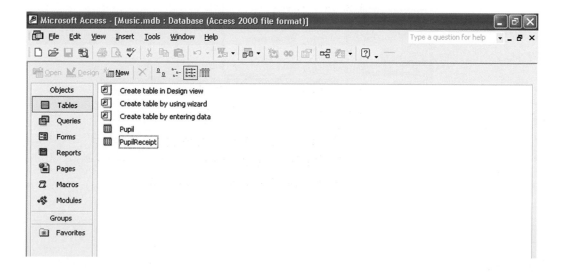

1 To set up a relationship between the two tables click on the relationships icon.

The Relationships window will open.

2 Add each table to the Relationships window.

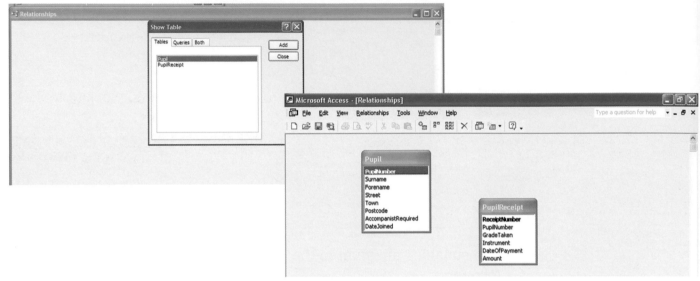

A relationship can be set up between the two tables. PupilNumber occurs in both tables therefore we will set a relationship up between the two tables on the field PupilNumber.

3 Do this by dragging PupilNumber from the Pupil table and dropping it on top of PupilNumber in the PupilReceipt table.

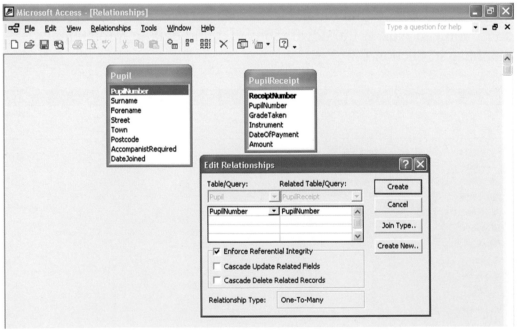

The *Edit Relationships* window will appear.

4 Tick the "*Enforce Referential Integrity*" check box.

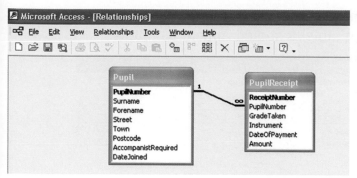

This means that only a pupil number which is in the Pupil table will be accepted in the PupilReceipt table.

Since one pupil studies many instruments the Relationship Type is One-To-Many.

5 Close the *Edit Relationships* window.
6 Close the *Relationships* window.
7 Save the changes to the Relationships.

■ Add data to the PupilReceipt table

1 Create a form for entering the new data into the PupilReceipt table.
2 Enter the following data into the PupilReceipt table:

ReceiptNumber	PupilNumber	GradeTaken	Instrument	DateOfPayment	Amount
1	1000	Grade 5	Violin	12-Sep-04	£40.00
2	1020	Grade 4	Piano	14-Sep-04	£24.00
3	1021	Grade 4	Piano	05-Oct-04	£24.00
4	1005	Grade 6	Flute	12-Sep-04	£50.00
5	1000	Grade 5	Piano	15-Sep-04	£30.00
6	1005	Grade 6	Violin	15-Sep-04	£47.00
7	1005	Grade 4	Piano	05-Oct-04	£24.00
8	1006	Grade 5	Flute	15-Sep-04	£35.00
9	1010	Grade 4	Violin	05-Oct-04	£28.00
10	1019	Grade 6	Piano	14-Sep-04	£55.00
11	1020	Grade 5	Flute	12-Sep-04	£35.00
12	1028	Grade 5	Violin	21-Sep-04	£40.00
13	1028	Grade 4	Flute	14-Sep-04	£22.00
14	1023	Grade 6	Flute	12-Oct-04	£45.00
15	1009	Grade 4	Piano	05-Oct-04	£24.00
16	1000	Grade 4	Piano	14-Sep-04	£24.00
17	1011	Grade 5	Piano	19-Oct-04	£30.00
18	1014	Grade 4	Violin	05-Oct-04	£28.00
19	1013	Grade 6	Flute	19-Oct-04	£45.00
20	1023	Grade 4	Piano	14-Sep-04	£24.00

3 Save the PupilReceipt table.

4 View the PupilReceipt table. It should appear as follows:

ReceiptNumber	PupilNumber	GradeTaken	Instrument	DateOfPayment	Amount
1	1000	Grade 5	Violin	12-Sep-04	£40.00
2	1020	Grade 4	Piano	14-Sep-04	£24.00

5 View the Pupil table.

A relationship has been set up between these two tables so the related records in the PupilReceipt table are visible.

Ellen Black has paid for three examinations.

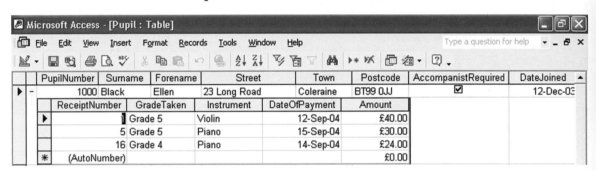

PupilNumber	Surname	Forename	Street	Town	Postcode	AccompanistRequired	DateJoined
1000	Black	Ellen	23 Long Road	Coleraine	BT99 0JJ	☑	12-Dec-03

ReceiptNumber	GradeTaken	Instrument	DateOfPayment	Amount
1	Grade 5	Violin	12-Sep-04	£40.00
5	Grade 5	Piano	15-Sep-04	£30.00
16	Grade 4	Piano	14-Sep-04	£24.00
(AutoNumber)				£0.00

Querying a database

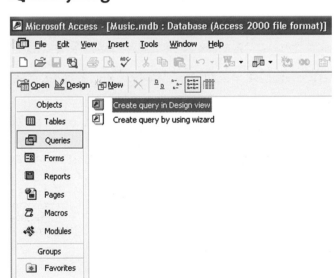

In a computerised database many records can be searched and information can be retrieved very quickly. Microsoft Access provides a Query facility. This allows users to ask the database to find records which fit certain criteria.

1 To create a query, click on the Queries tab.

2 Select *Create query in Design view*.

Ruth wishes to make a list of all the pupils who require an accompanist. All of this information can be found from the Pupil table.

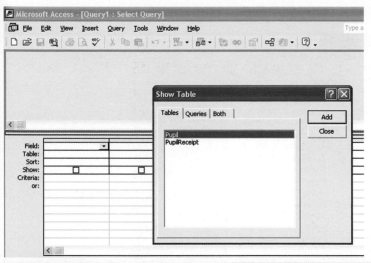

The *Show Table* window will appear.

3 Add the Pupil Table and close the *Show Table* window.

4 Add the following fields to the Query Design window by double-clicking on them:
- Surname.
- Forename.
- Street.
- Town.
- Postcode.
- Accompanist Required.

5 Type "Yes" into the Criteria row of the AccompanistRequired column.

The pupils who require an accompanist will have the value "Yes" in the AccompanistRequired field.

6 Uncheck the Show box in the AccompanistRequired column.

This means that this field will not be shown in the results of the query.

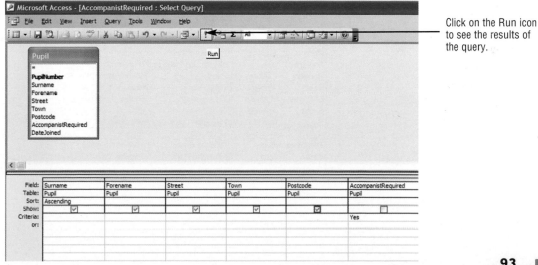

Click on the Run icon to see the results of the query.

The results are shown in table format.

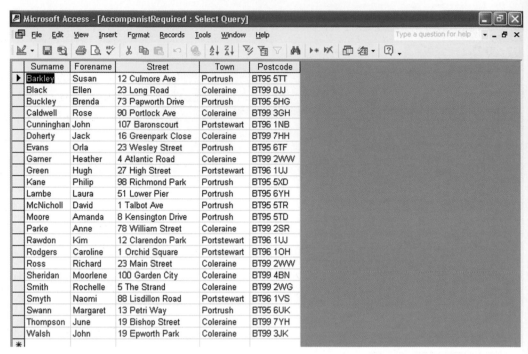

23 pupils out of 31 require an accompanist to play while they are taking their exam.

7 Save the query as AccompanistRequired.

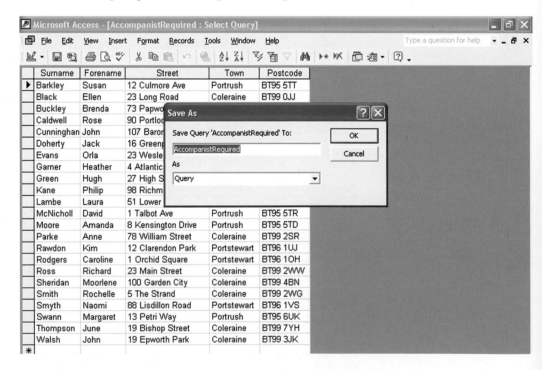

■ Creating queries which require more than one table

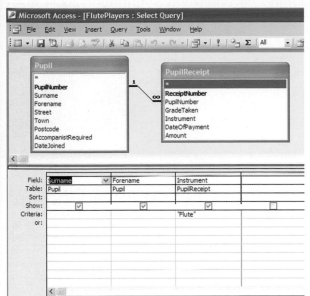

One of the main advantages of linking (or relating) two tables is that data from both tables can be used at the same time.

Ruth has a question. She wants to produce a list of names of all those pupils who have paid for Flute exams. In order to do this data from both tables is required.

1 Create a new query in Design view.
2 Add both tables to the Query Design window.
3 Add Surname and Forename from the Pupil table.
4 Add Instrument from the PupilReceipt table.
5 To search for all Flute players type "Flute" into the Criteria row of the Instrument column.
6 Run the query.
7 View the results.
8 Save the query as FlutePlayers.

Six people have payed for Flute examinations.

■ Creating queries using logical operators and more than one criteria

Logical operators are words like AND and OR which allow us to combine conditions.

Ruth needs answers to the following questions. The questions are outlined and the way in which the queries are designed are shown. Using the details create the three queries and show the output you have generated from each.

Query 1
Who are the pupils who play the flute AND need an accompanist?

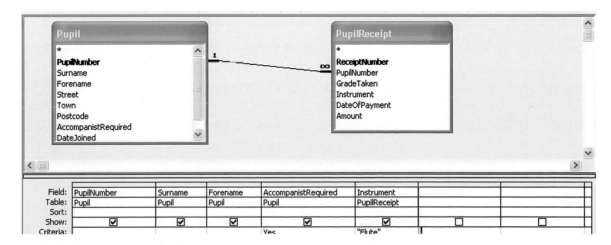

Query 2

Who are the pupils who have joined between 1st September 2004 and today?

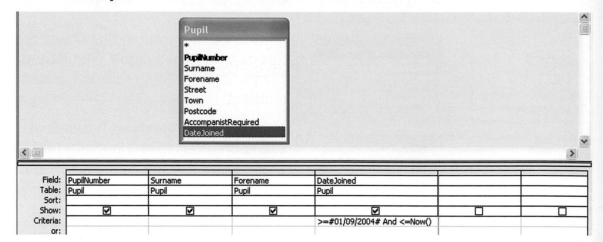

Query 3

Who are the pupils who have paid to take Grade 5 in violin or piano?

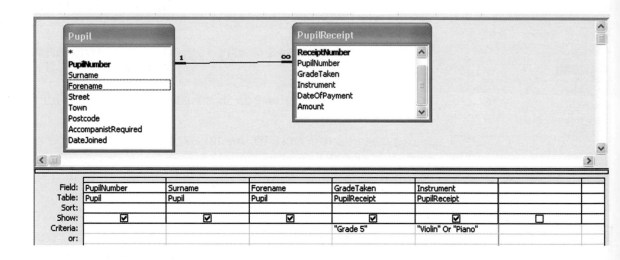

Reports

Reports allow us to present information obtained from a database so that it can be easily read and understood.

Ruth wants to produce a list showing what each of her students have paid for.

To do this she will need to design a report. Like queries, reports can make use of one or two tables.

1 Select *Create a report by using wizard.*

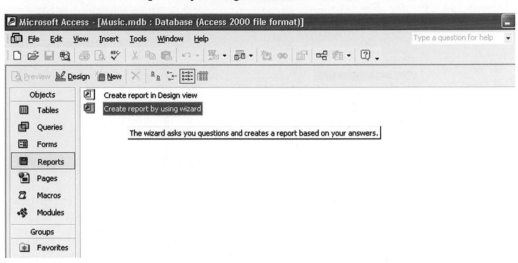

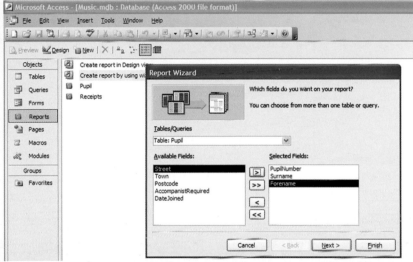

The *Report Wizard* window will open.

2 Select the Pupil table.
3 Add the PupilNumber, Surname and Forename fields to the Selected Fields list.

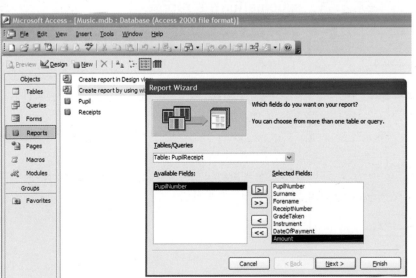

4 Select the PupilReceipt table.
5 Add the ReceiptNumber, GradeTaken, Instrument, DateOfPayment and Amount fields to the Selected Fields list.
6 Click **Next**.

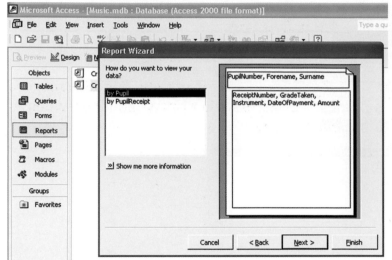

Ruth wishes to view the data in order of pupil number.

7 Select *By Pupil*. Click **Next**.

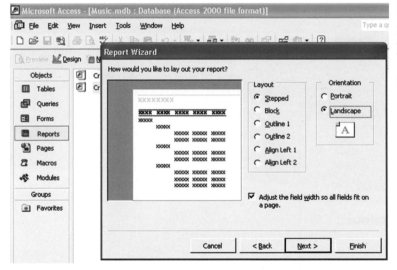

Since there will be so many fields on the report, it is best to select **Landscape** layout.

8 Click **Next**.

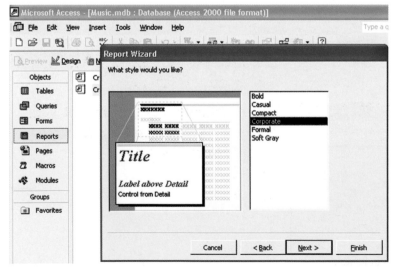

You can also select a style and colour scheme for the report.

9 Select *Corporate*. Click **Next**.

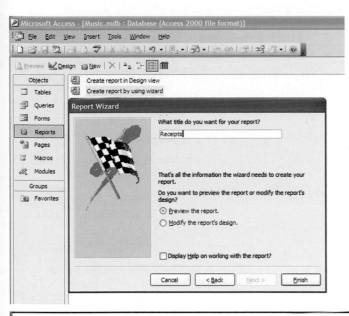

This is the last stage in producing the report using the wizard.

10 Save the report as *Receipts*.

If the *Preview the report* radio button is selected Microsoft Access will display the report when *Finish* is clicked.

This is a section of the finished report showing the examinations which each pupil has paid for:

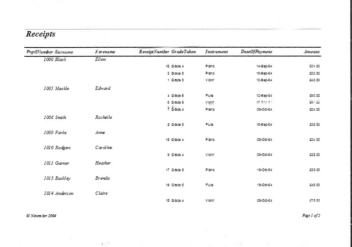

▪ Extension activity

Some improvements could be made to the report by viewing it in design layout.

1 To view the report in design layout click on the **Design View** icon.

2 Change the report heading to *Pupil Bill Details* as shown.

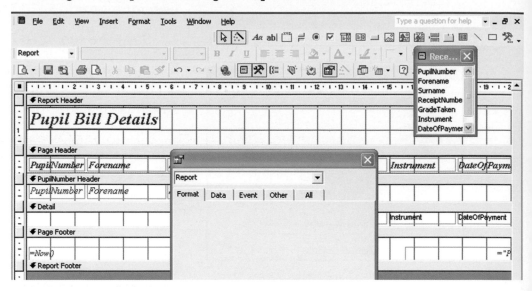

3 Save the report.

Ruth has decided that she would like to place the total amount paid by each pupil after their details on the report.

4 Open Receipts in Design View.
5 Select View.
6 Select Sorting and Grouping.

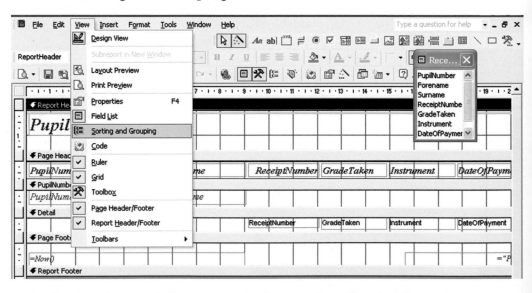

7 In the *Sorting and Grouping* window, select **Yes** for Group Footer.

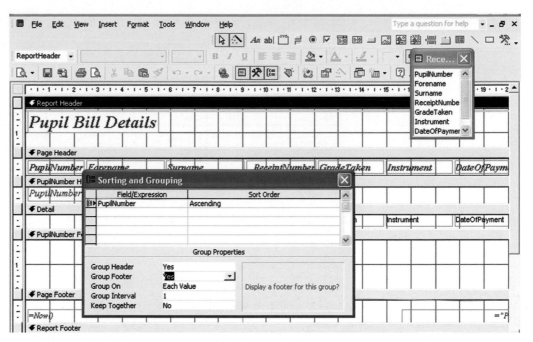

A new area will appear on the report called PupilNumber Footer.

8　Add a textbox to this area.

9　Place the textbox in line with the Amount field.

10　Press F4 to view the properties associated with the textbox.

11　Click on the **Data** tab.

12　In Control Source place the formula =SUM (Amount). This will total the amount paid for each pupil.

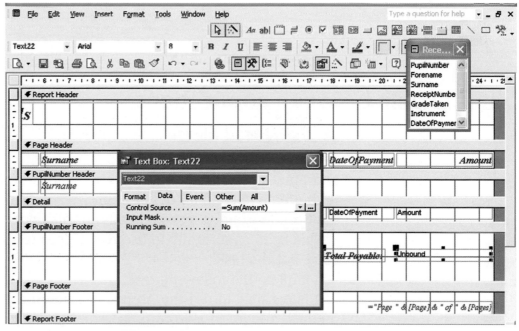

13　Click on the **Format** tab.

14　Select Currency from the drop-down list.

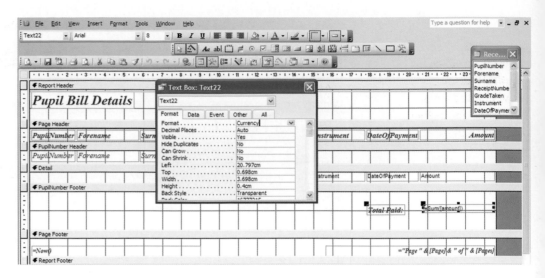

15 Save the report.

16 View the report before printing.

The figure shows a section of the report showing a subtotal for each pupil.

Sharing data between applications

■ Using Mail Merge

Any music pupil who requires an accompanist must come to a meeting and practise with their chosen accompanist on Friday 29th January. Ruth wants to send all of her pupils, who require an accompanist for their grade exam, a letter containing this information.

This is an opportunity to use two pieces of software to help Ruth carry out the task.

Complete the following task:

It is possible to use the AccompanistRequired query created earlier to produce a letter in a word processor. The Mail Merge facility in the word processor can merge the query contents with the letter. This creates an individual letter for each pupil.

1 Create the main letter with the information, using a word processor.

This letter, called **mailletter.doc** can be downloaded from www.hoddernorthernireland.co.uk/ict/

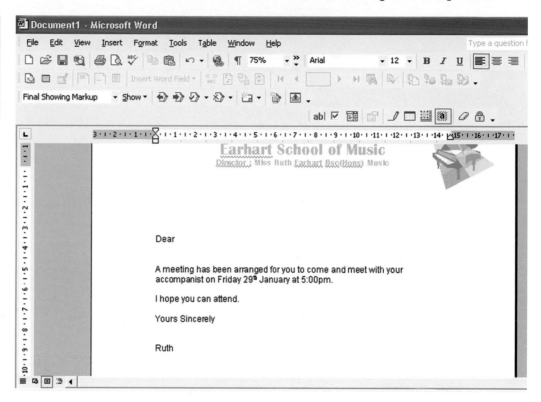

2 Attach the AccompanistRequired query to the main letter by selecting the Mail Merge option in the word processor.

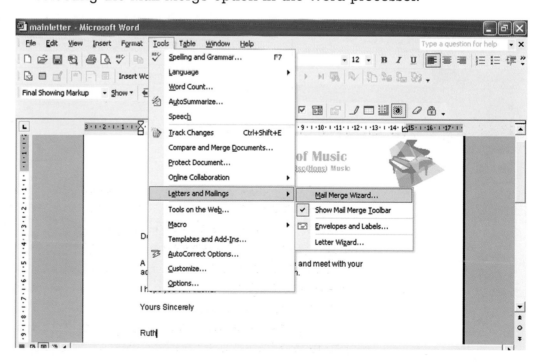

3 Select the document type. Click on the **Letters** radio button as shown.

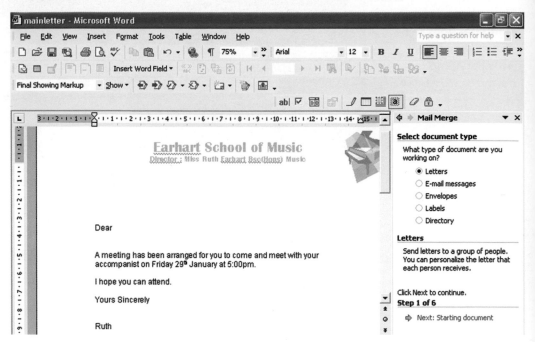

4 Select the starting document. Click on the **Use the current document** radio button.

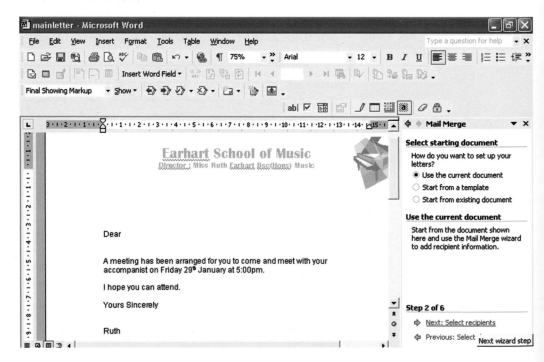

5 Select the recipients. Click on the **Use an existing list** radio button.

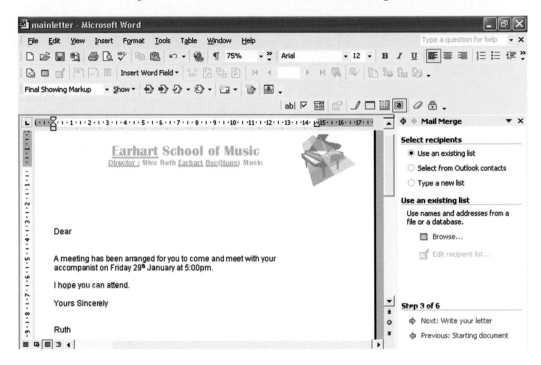

The *Select Data Source* window will open.

6 Click to open the database file *Music.mdb*.

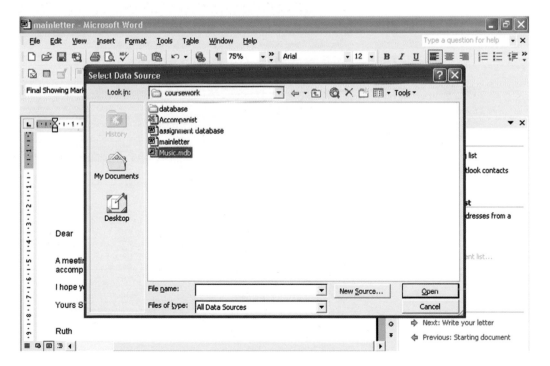

The *Select Table* window will appear.

7 Click to select the AccompanistRequired query.

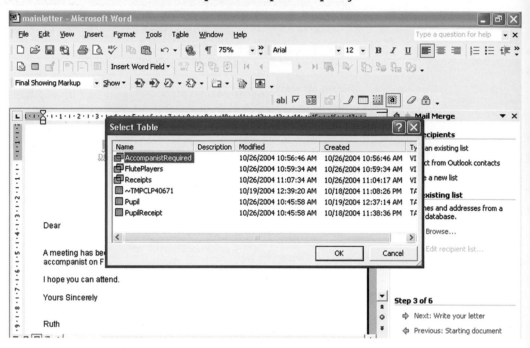

The *Mail Merge Recipients* window will appear.

8 Click **Select All** to include all of the fields in the merged letter.

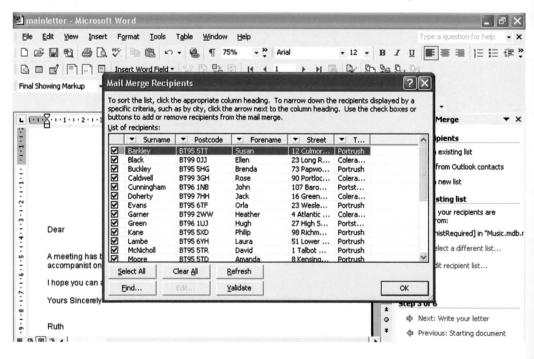

9 Using the Insert Merge Fields Icon, position the fields onto the letter.

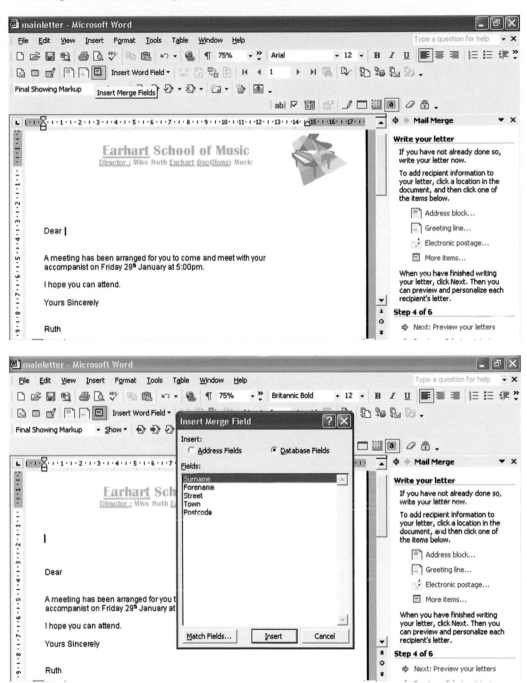

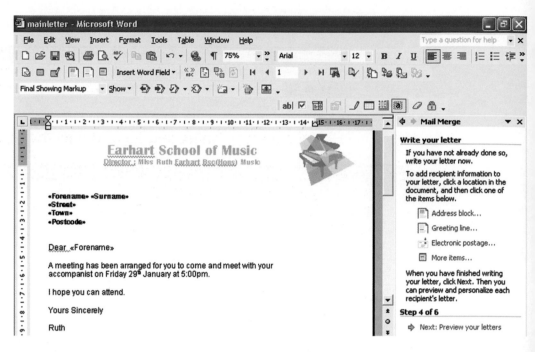

Note that merge fields are shown inside brackets << and >>. It is easy to identify where the data will appear on the letters.

10 Merge the main letter with the data to produce individual letters.

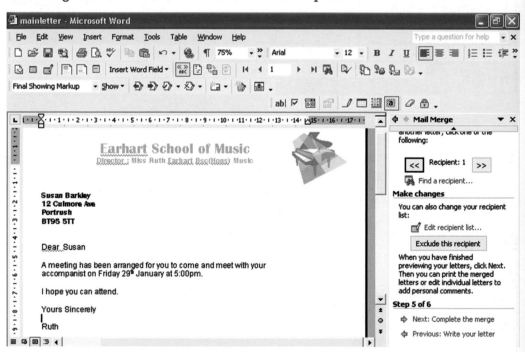

11 Print the individualised letters.

■ Importing files from another source

Ruth has created a list of possible accompanists and the instruments that they play. She has done this in a spreadsheet. She wishes to import the details in the spreadsheet into the database for use in queries.

1 Create a spreadsheet and enter the following data:

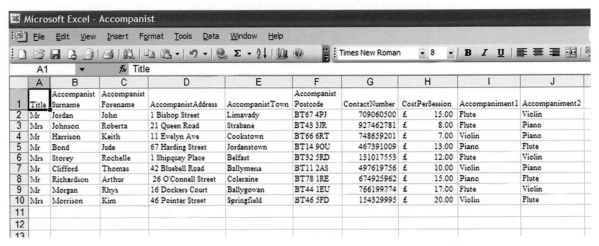

> Alternatively the digital version of the file *Accompanist.xls* can be used to complete this exercise.

To import the data into a table, open the Access database *Music.mdb*.

1 Select File.
2 Select Get External Data.
3 Select Import. . . .

The *Import* window will open.

4 Go to the **Files of type** box and select *Microsoft Excel*.
5 Click on the file **Accompanist**.
6 Click **Import**.

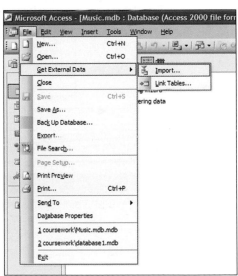

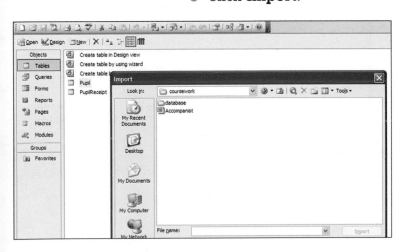

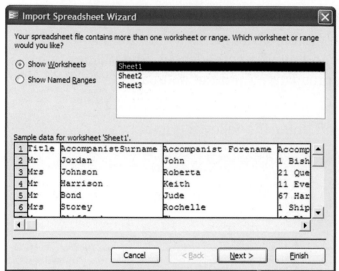

The Import Spreadsheet Wizard appears.

7 Click **Next.**

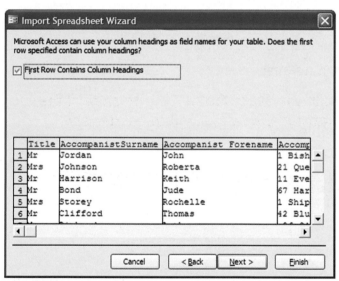

8 On the next screen, tick the check box *First Row Contains Column Headings.*
9 Click **Next**.
10 Select the option to store data *In a New Table.*
11 Click **Next**.

12 Click **Next** at the next screen, to import all the fields.

13 Allow Access to allocate a primary key.

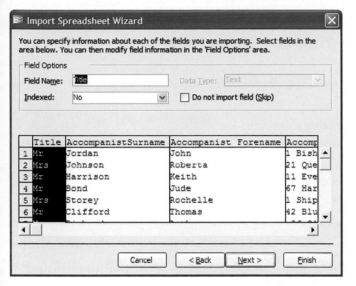

14 Import the table to Accompanist.

A new table will now exist in the list of tables. The structure of the new table is shown. This table can now be used in queries and reports.

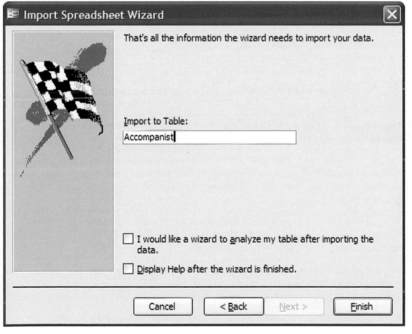

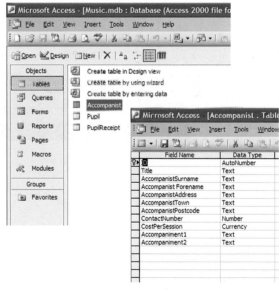

8 Spreadsheet packages C1(h)

▶ **In this section you will learn about spreadsheets.**
Through examples you will gain skills which will assist in:

- Entering text and numbers.
- Formatting cells, rows and columns including conditional formatting and validation.
- Entering formulae and replicating formulae.
- Creating, labelling and formatting charts.

▶ **This is assessed through the following components:**

- Terminal examination(s).
- Assignment B3: Spreadsheet(s).

This section is supported by the following digital media which may be accessed through www.hoddernorthern ireland.co.uk/ict/
GCSE Coursework marks – EXCEL File
Lookup Table – EXCEL file

Spreadsheet packages have a number of common features as outlined in the table below.

Feature	Detail of feature
Cell	Cells can store data in the form of text, number, date, formula or reference to another cell.
Cell format	Cells can be formatted by changing font size and style. Also cells can be given borders or shaded to emphasise appearance. You can also format data in cells. For example the date can be formatted to DDMMYY.
Columns and rows	The user can vary the width of columns and alter the height of cells.
Locking cells	Cells can be protected (read only) which means the user can not change the data. Cells can also be hidden to assist in security.
Fill	A formula or value can be entered into a cell and can be automatically replicated down or across.
Mathematical functions	The user can select from a choice of inbuilt mathematical functions. Some of the common functions include SUM, AVERAGE, MIN and MAX .
Graphs and charts	Data entered into the spreadsheet can be displayed on a graph or chart. The user can choose a 2-D or 3-D image and can also select from a variety of chart types. Once the user has selected the data to be entered into the chart the computer will automatically draw the chart.
Conditions	This is an advanced feature which allows the user to create a condition and control possible actions by using an expression such as: IF (condition) THEN (action) ELSE (action).
Lookup tables	Another advanced feature is a Lookup table. These tables contain data that can continuously be referenced using a lookup function. The function can use a Vlookup (vertical reference) or a Hlookup (horizontal lookup).
Macros	Some experienced users can write small programs referred to as macros. This involves the user creating a series of commands that can be performed by the spreadsheet automatically.

Microsoft Excel is an example of a spreadsheet package.

Entry of text and numbers

Spreadsheets are mainly designed to perform calculations and recalculations automatically. A spreadsheet consists of a table divided into rows and columns to produce cells. Cells have a column reference (letter) and a row reference (number).

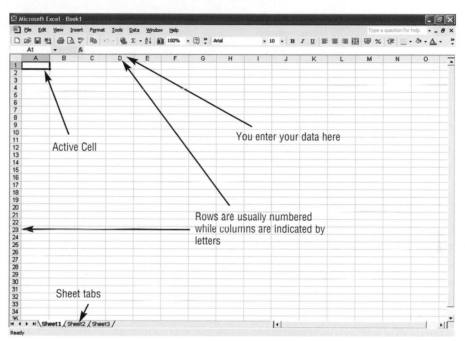

The contents of the **active cell,** are displayed in the formula bar. The column and row reference are also indicated, such as B4. Remember the column reference (a letter) is always first when referring to a cell.

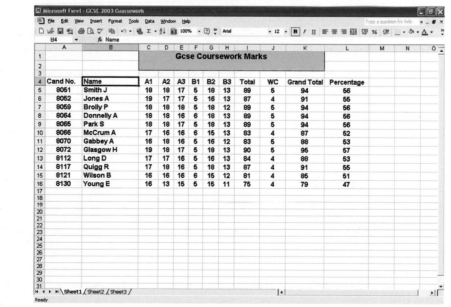

In spreadsheet section, crop empty folios of sheet if necessary to fit page.

■ To select a **row or column**, click on the row number or column letter, such as J.

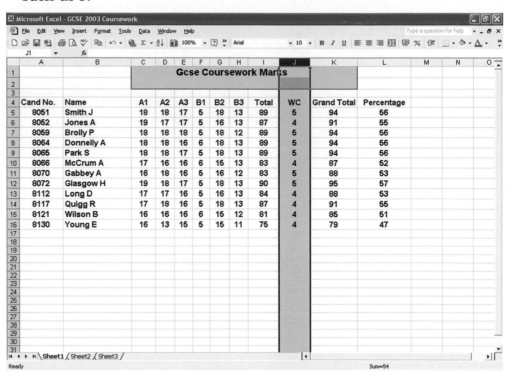

By moving the cursor to the point where column I ends and column J begins allows the user to alter the width of the column. This allows the user to insert and view a larger number of characters. The same process can be applied to rows.

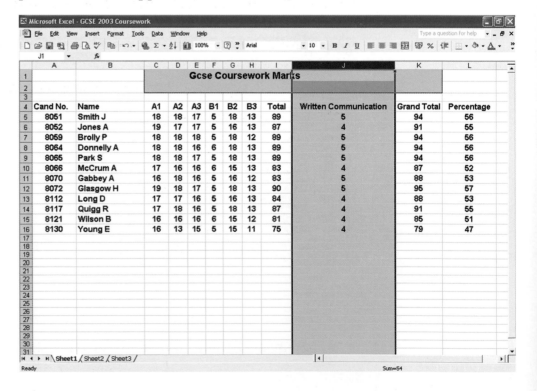

When entering data into a spreadsheet, you can format the data into a specified category such as:

- Number
- Currency
- Date

- Time
- Percentage
- Text

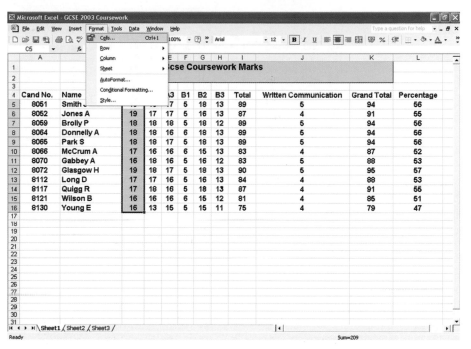

Formatting cells

Selecting the **Format** menu and the option **Cells**... allows the selected cells to be formatted.

Formatting cells allows the user to control the contents of a cell such as cell type and colour of font.

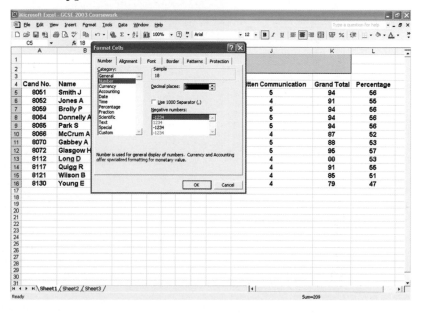

You can also format your spreadsheet to change its appearance.

1 Select cells referenced by columns A and B, and rows 5 to 16.

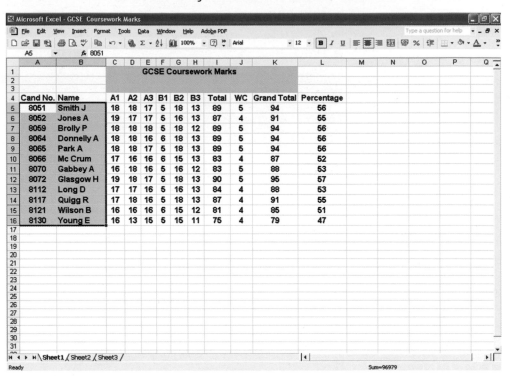

2 Then select from the **Format** option the option *Cells…* .

Changing the **format** will only apply to the selected cells.

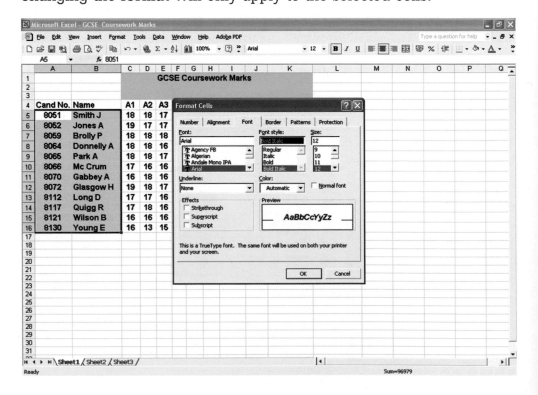

Remember to select the cells before formatting from the **Format** menu.

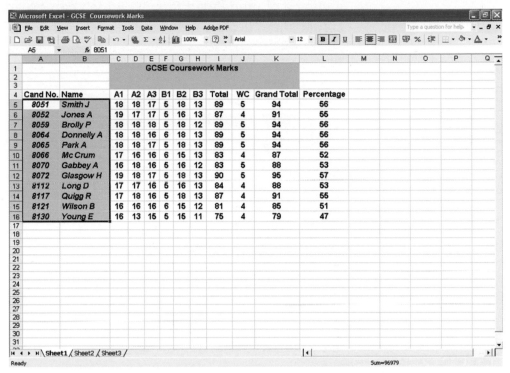

The **Format** menu and the option Cell … will also allow you to select borders and patterns. You can also select colours for your data and your cells.

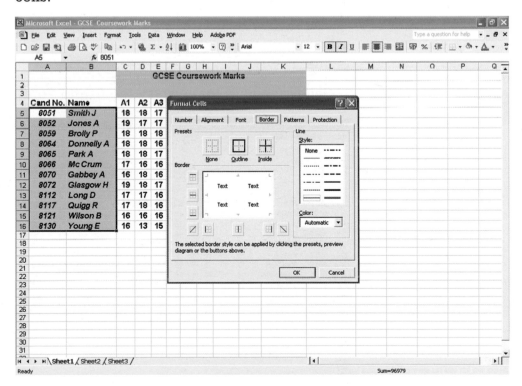

By selecting the **Format** menu, you can select *AutoFormat* which allows a choice of predefined formats which can be applied to the overall spreadsheet design.

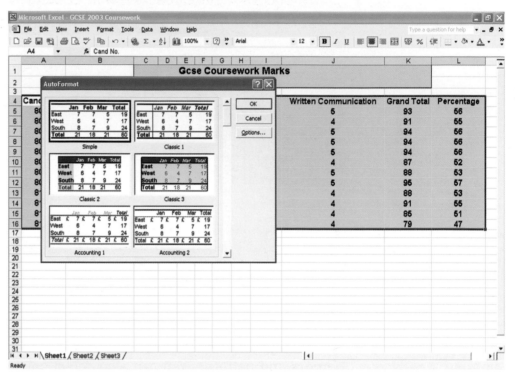

■ Conditional formatting

Conditional formatting allows the user to incorporate aspects such as cell shading or font colour automatically to cells if a specified condition is true.

1 Select the cells that display the **Grand Total.**

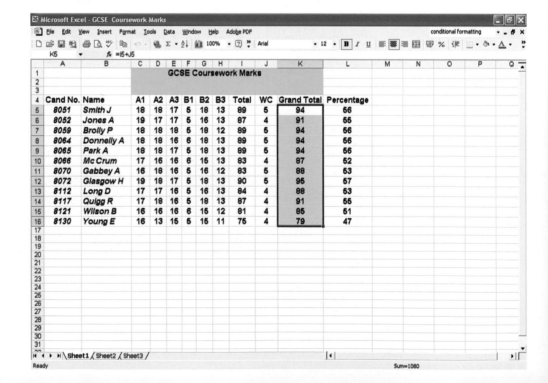

We want to display any score between 92 and 100 in a different font colour.

2 Select **Format** menu and the option *Conditional Formatting…* .

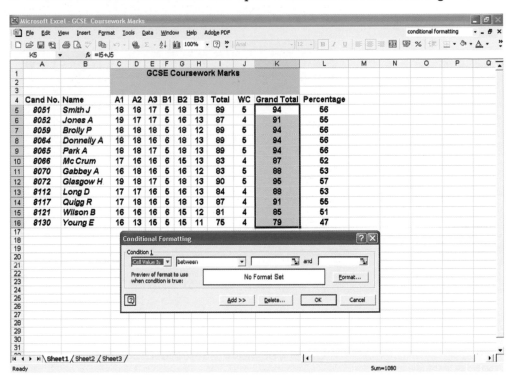

3 Enter the values 92 and 100 in the Conditional formatting dialog box.

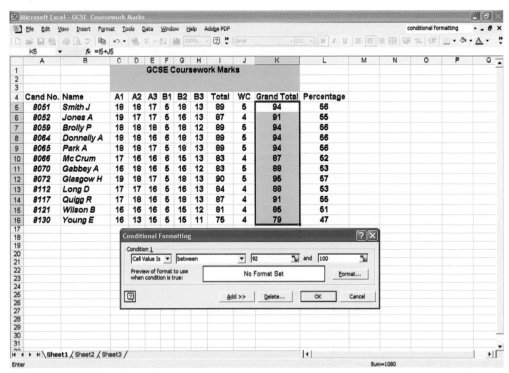

4 By clicking on **Format**, select a suitable font colour such as red.

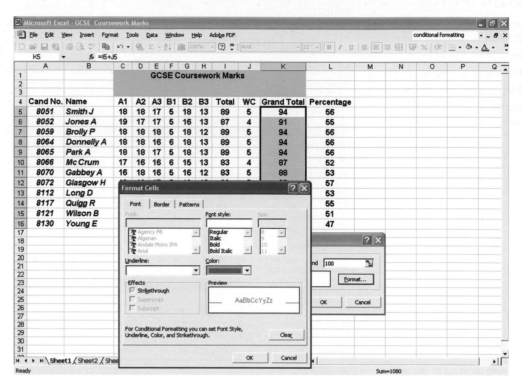

5 Once you have selected the colour click **OK**.

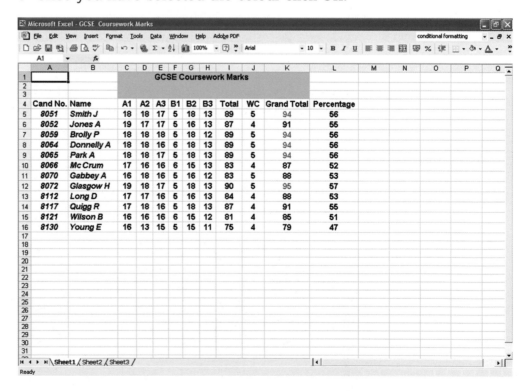

Data validation in spreadsheets

Note, you can also set the acceptable data type. In this case the number will be defined as a whole number.

It is possible to control the value allowed in a given cell. By selecting the **Data** menu and then the option *Validation…* a dialog box will appear. If you consider the assignment A1, the maximum mark achievable is 19. Therefore you can select a range between 1 and 19 as your validation check.

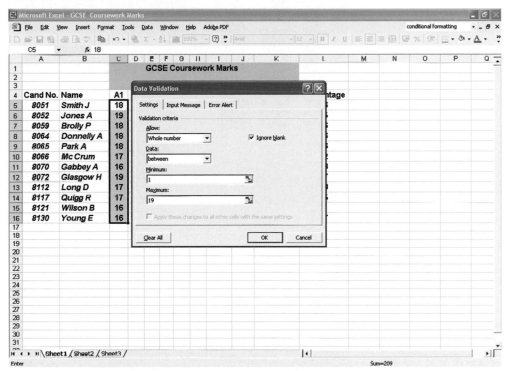

You can also enter a suitable message to guide the user by selecting the **Input Message** tab, and then entering your message.

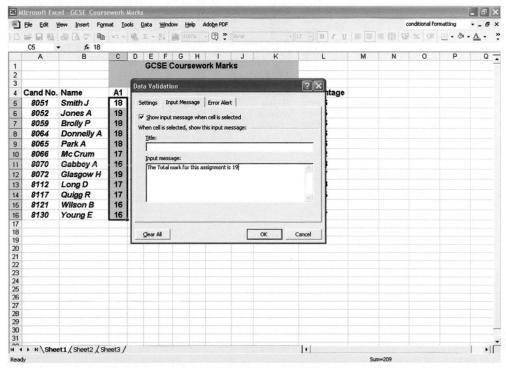

By using the **Error Alert** tab you can control the style of the error message by selecting *stop, warning* or *information.*

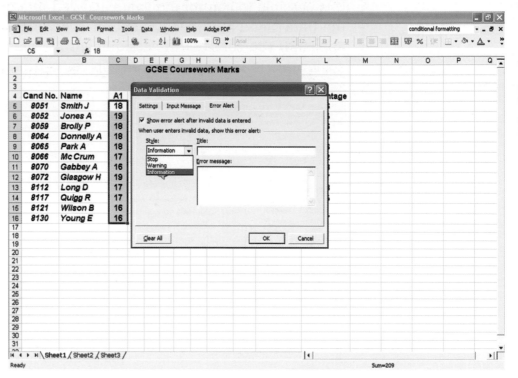

If you alter a value in the spreadsheet and input a higher value than 19 for assignment A1, the error message created will be displayed.

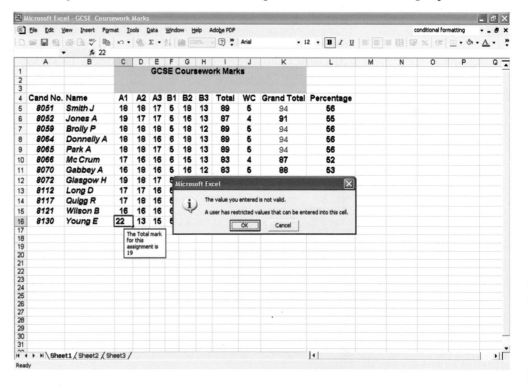

Entry of formulae and replicating formulae

To enter a simple formulae you start with an equals sign (=) followed by the formula, such as I5 + J5 to add written communication to the total mark for the assignments.

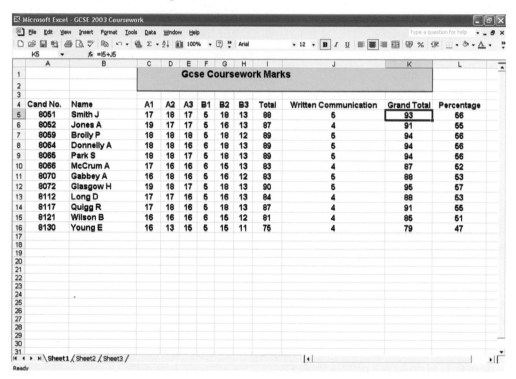

Selecting the **Edit** menu and the options *Fill* and *Down* allows the formulae to be replicated in the selected column.

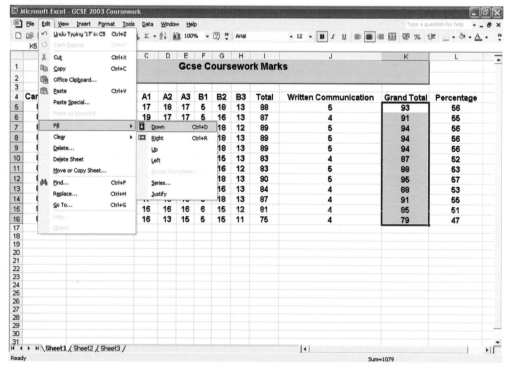

▶ You need to learn the definitions of these terms:

- Peripheral device
- External memory
- Internal memory
- Control unit
- Main memory
- Arithmetic and Logic Unit
- Random Access Memory
- Read Only Memory
- Booting up program
- Data Bus
- Cache memory
- Function key

- Control key
- Shift key
- Cursor key
- Hot key
- Character transposition error
- Omission error
- Transcription error
- Digital data
- email
- Voice mail
- Sensor resolution
- Soft copy

- Hard copy
- Pixel
- Disk formatting
- Tracks and sectors
- Multimedia
- Random access
- Serial access
- File backup
- File archive
- File recovery

▶ You need to expand all of these acronyms:

- ASCII
- CPU
- VDU
- CD-ROM
- DVD
- VDU
- ALU

- RAM
- ROM
- MB
- kB
- GB
- EPOS
- ATM

- LCD
- DPI
- OCR
- PDA
- SVGA
- CPS
- PPM

- CD-R
- CD-RW
- WORM
- RTF
- WYSIWYG
- GUI
- WIMP

A typical home computer has a number of components. These can be put into categories such as:

- Central Processing Unit (e.g. Pentium 4)
- Input devices (e.g. keyboard)
- Output devices (e.g. VDU)
- Storage devices (e.g. DVD drive)

▶ Typical home computer components

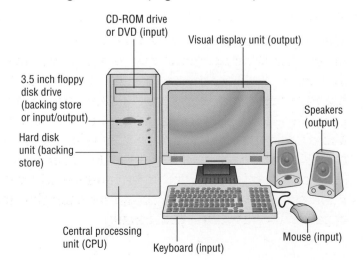

CD-ROM drive or DVD (input)

Visual display unit (output)

3.5 inch floppy disk drive (backing store or input/output)

Hard disk unit (backing store)

Speakers (output)

Central processing unit (CPU)

Keyboard (input)

Mouse (input)

The diagram shows how the components are related.

▶ Relationship of
components

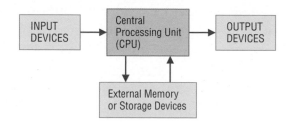

A Brief Overview of the CPU

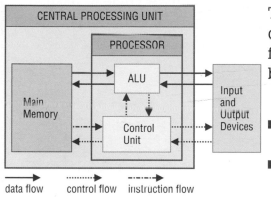

data flow   control flow   instruction flow

▲ The CPU

The CPU is sometimes referred to as the *brain* of the computer. However, unlike the human brain it cannot think for itself. It requires humans to supply programs and data before it can process.

A typical CPU consists of three main elements:

- Control Unit – responsible for co-ordinating the Input and Output devices and all related activities.
- Arithmetic and Logic Unit (ALU) – Calculations are done here and logical decisions are made.
- Main Memory – Holds the programs and data that are currently being used.

■ The main memory

The CPU contains two different types of memories. Both of these memories are often referred to as firmware because they use microchips.

- RAM (Random Access Memory)
- ROM (Read Only Memory)

■ RAM (Random Access Memory)

▲ Memory chips

This type of memory can be read from or written to. It is volatile which means the contents of the memory are lost when the machine is switched off. The contents can be changed as the need arises such as the user using a different type of application program. It is used to hold programs and data that the user is using such as Microsoft Windows, Microsoft Word and an ICT Assignment. All programs and data including the ones currently in RAM are held in permanent memory such as a Hard Disk. Typical RAM size is 512 MB. The size of RAM can influence the speed of the processor such that the larger the RAM capacity the faster the processing.

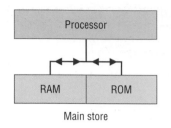

▲ Memory organisation

■ ROM (Read Only Memory)

This type of memory can be read from but not written to. Programs stored on ROM are permanent which means the contents cannot be altered. Therefore if we describe RAM as volatile then ROM is non-volatile. They are used to store programs that are frequently required by the computer such as the "booting up" program for Windows.

This program runs automatically when the computer is turned on to load the operating system (such as Windows XP).

■ Cache memory

This is a special type of memory. It is part of the CPU and is located between the processor and the main memory. Cache memory is usually smaller in capacity than main memory and data stored here can be accessed much faster by the CPU. This speeds up the time it takes for the computer to complete an instruction. Cache is a form of random access memory and the processor will check cache memory for data before checking the main memory.

Input Devices

■ Keyboards

When you purchase a computer system you receive a keyboard. Most manufacturers use a standard layout (referred to as QWERTY) on their keyboards.

▶ A typical keyboard

The following table summarises the types of keys on a standard keyboard.

When using a keyboard the speed of Input depends on the human operator. Compared to other input devices they are considered to be slow. Due to the amount of human involvement there is a tendency for human errors to occur. These are described as transcription errors.

Keys	Description
Alphabet	Keys produce lowercase (small letters) or uppercase (capital letters). The *Shift* or *Caps Lock* keys allow the user to type in uppercase only.
Digits 0–9	Appear twice: once along the top of the keyboard and as a separate keypad to the right.
Alphanumeric	These can refer to letters and/or digits and combinations of these.
Other characters	Punctuation marks (,: ; ' " ") Mathematical and other symbols (% $ £ < +)
Cursor and Control Characters	Arrow keys, TAB, Page Up/Down Editing Keys (insert, delete) Control Keys (Enter (or Return), Escape)
Function Keys	Labelled F1, F2, F3, etc. The function of these keys is normally set by the program currently being used.
Keys which change the function of other keys	Keys marked SHIFT, CAPS LOCK, NUM LOCK, ALT, CTRL

Eject
Display
Clear

Play
Pause
FF
Stop
REW

▲ A typical remote control

Some keyboards are specially designed for certain applications. The layout of keys would be dedicated to the needs of the application such as automated teller machines (ATMs) and electronic point of sale (EPOS) terminals. These keyboards may have fewer keys with emphasis on numeric keys.

At home we use a lot of keyboard type devices such as remote controls for our televisions.

In schools some teachers use Concept Keyboards where the keys are labelled as pictures or words. Teachers can use overlays on Concept Keyboards to change the words and pictures. The keys are therefore sometimes described as programmable keys. Concept keyboards are also used in supermarket fruit and vegetable departments for customers to weigh their own purchases. They are also used on vending machines.

▶ A concept keyboard

■ Mouse

A mouse is also referred to as a *pointing device*. It is designed to fit the human hand and when moved produces movements of a pointer on a VDU. A roller ball moves inbuilt sensors which pick up the movements and send corresponding signals back to the computer.

A mouse has two or three buttons which are used to make selections on the screen. The left-hand button is used to make selections such as selecting options from menus, selecting icons and positioning the cursor on the screen. The right-hand button is used to display shortcut menus at the position of the cursor.

This device is considered easy to use and inexpensive to purchase compared to other input devices. One drawback is that experienced users find it slow compared to using *hot keys*. For example they prefer to press Ctrl and P to print rather than selecting menus and options.

Modern mice use technology such as infrared or wireless links which eliminates the need for the user connecting it to the computer by cable. A tracker ball is an alternative to a mouse.

▲ A tracker ball

■ Joystick

A joystick is an input device which allows the user to control the movement of the cursor on the screen by manoeuvring a small lever in different directions. The lever can be moved in any direction, for example side to side, up and down and diagonally.

Like a mouse it uses inbuilt sensors to convert the movements into co-ordinates on the screen. Joysticks usually have buttons to allow actions to be carried out. The main use of a joystick is in the playing of computer games (in this context is may be referred to as a *games paddle*). They are also used to move computer controlled devices such as robots and hospital scanners.

▲ A joystick

■ Tracker pad

This input device is also known as a *touch sensitive pad*. It is used as an alternative to a mouse on a laptop computer due to space restrictions. The pad can sense the touch from a finger by recognising the change in temperature. Moving your finger on the pad allows you to control the cursor which in turn will allow you to select options from menus, select icons and position the cursor. Tapping the touch pad is equivalent to clicking the left-hand mouse button. The touch pad is very sensitive and therefore can be more difficult to use initially than a mouse.

▶ A taptop touchpad

■ Microphone

This device is designed to input sound, such as human voice, into a computer system. This type of system is referred to as a *voice recognition system.* These systems can convert sound to text or accept spoken commands. The recognition rate can be low and inaccurate particularly if there is background noise. Voice recognition can be successful when a user trains the computer to recognise their voice by storing words and phrases they use. Microphones are also used to record music and store it in digital format in the computer.

The microphone is used as an input device for voice mail which works like email except a voice message is left rather than a text message. It is also used in applications that only require a limited number of words or phrases such as telephone banking.

■ Digital camera

A digital camera can store many more pictures than an ordinary camera. The picture taken by the digital camera is stored on a memory card as opposed to film in an ordinary camera. A typical memory card can hold 512 MB which allows around 200 pictures to be stored in medium resolution or quality. Most digital cameras have a small liquid crystal display (LCD) screen which can display the picture(s) taken immediately. This allows the user the options of storing or deleting the image taken.

Pictures can be downloaded from the camera to a computer from where they can be printed or edited using a graphics software package. The cost of printing the images in different sizes onto photograph paper is much cheaper than developing a film. The cost will vary depending on the type of paper used. Full glossy photographic paper can be expensive compared to a matt finished paper.

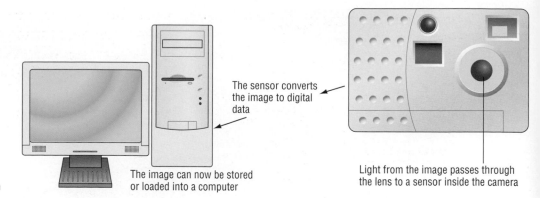

The sensor converts the image to digital data

The image can now be stored or loaded into a computer

Light from the image passes through the lens to a sensor inside the camera

▶ Using a digital camera

Advanced digital cameras can also capture short video clips that last a couple of minutes but for longer videos a digital video camera is required. Pictures taken by digital cameras are in digital form and so they can be transmitted by email immediately.

■ Scanner

A scanner can be used to input pictures and text from a hard copy format into a computer. There are two types of scanners available. The most commonly used is the flat-bed scanner. The other type which is hand-held is best suited for scanning 3-D objects. Hand-held scanners tend to be portable and cheap but the scanned image is not as high quality as that of a flat-bed scanner.

Flat-bed scanners are normally A4 in size but you can purchase bigger scanners that can scan images such as A3 size. Scanners work by passing beams of bright light over the image. The image is recognised as a large number of dots on a page. The quality of the image scanned is measured in dots per inch (dpi). Cheap scanners can scan at 2400 dpi but only up to A4 in size.

The greater the dpi, the greater the resolution or quality of the image scanned. The drawback of high quality resolution is the greater amount of memory required to store the image.

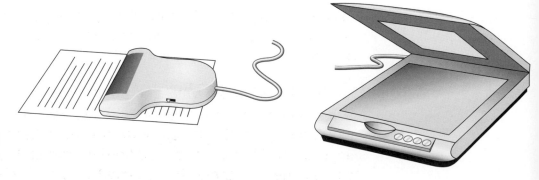

▶ A hand-held and flat-bed scanner

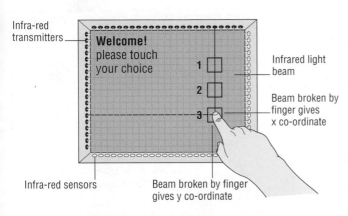

Infra-red transmitters

Welcome! please touch your choice

Infrared light beam

Beam broken by finger gives x co-ordinate

Infra-red sensors

Beam broken by finger gives y co-ordinate

▲ A touch screen schematic

▲ A typical touch screen

Once the image has been scanned it can be saved and changed using standard software. If text has been scanned it can be recognised as text on a word processor using optical character recognition (OCR) software. The user can then format the text, add to the text and even email the text.

■ Touch screen

Although it looks like an ordinary visual display unit (VDU) it is regarded as a special type of screen which reacts to human touch. Some of these screens operate using vertical and horizontal beams of infrared light just in front of the glass. When the user's finger touches the screen, vertical and horizontal beams of light are broken which convert into coordinates in the form of (x, y). Other screens work on the principle of heat, whereby the screen can sense a change of heat when the finger touches a part of the screen.

A touch screen is normally used in conjunction with a graphical user interface (GUI). Typically the user makes selections by touching the screen. They are commonly used in banks, tourist offices, museums and information kiosks. The user does not require much ICT competence compared with using a mouse or a keyboard which makes them attractive to use.

Output Devices

Output devices are used to provide results in a suitable format after data has been processed by a computer. Output formats are classified as one of two states: soft copy or hard copy. Soft copy output is described as a temporary copy of information such as information displayed on a screen while hard copy output is a permanent copy of information such as a printout.

■ Visual Display Units (VDUs)

Sometimes we refer to these devices loosely as *screens* or *display units* and formally as Visual Display Units (VDUs). Depending on the application VDUs come in all different sizes and shapes. For example on portable devices the VDU is a Liquid Crystal Display (LCD) screen. This type of screen is used on laptop computers and PDAs because they do not take up much space and they are not heavy which makes the computer portable. Apart from these advantages there are drawbacks. One drawback of LCD screens is that they cannot be viewed from different angles. Another drawback is the additional expense compared to ordinary desktop VDUs.

▶ a) Desktop PC with a Flat Screen;
b) Personal Digital Assistant;
c) Laptop computer

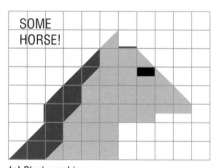

Microphone
Monitor
Screen size
Built-in speakers
Controls for brightness, horizontal/vertical shift, etc
On/off switch

▲ A typical VDU

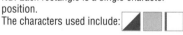

SOME HORSE!

(a) Block graphics

NB. Each rectangle is a single character position.
The characters used include:

Sketch of horse

(b) High resolution graphics

▲ Resolution

Visual Display Units differ from each other in size and resolution. The size of a VDU is measured in inches diagonally across the screen while the quality of the image displayed is referred to as resolution. Some applications use monochrome VDUs while other applications use coloured VDUs. Monochrome screens can only display one background and one foreground colour such as black and white. Colour monitors can display from 16 to a million different colours. When we purchase a new screen they are often referred to as multimedia VDUs because they are supplied with inbuilt speakers and even inbuilt microphones.

The quality and detail of a picture on a VDU depends on the resolution.

A pixel is square in shape and represents the smallest area on the screen the computer can change. Resolution is measured in pixels.

High resolution VDUs have a greater number of pixels than low resolution VDUs. Most home PCs come with a SVGA monitor with a resolution of 1024 × 768 pixels. Modern VDUs have an inbuilt filtering system to help with the problem of eyestrain. The higher the resolution and the bigger the VDU size means that the VDU's cost will increase.

■ Printers

There is a range of printers available. ICT users will purchase a printer depending on their needs. Typically a printer for a home computer costs less than £100. Apart from cost a user will consider other factors when purchasing a printer such as:

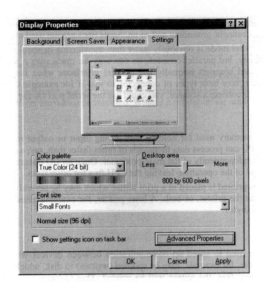

In windows the advanced user can control the appearance of their display by using *display properties*

► Changing display properties

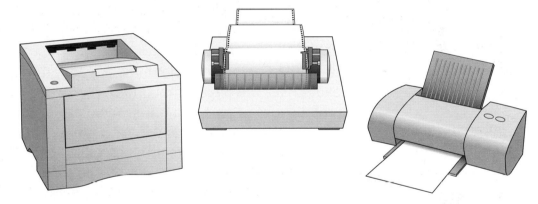

► Different types of printer

- Quality of print (dots per inch).
- Speed of the printer (characters per second/pages per minute).
- Colour or black and white printing capability.
- Ability to print text and graphics.
- Size of paper that can be used such as A4 and A3.
- Type of paper that can be used such as photographic paper.
- Volume of printing required.
- Cost of the consumables such as the replacement ink kits.

Ink-jet printers

These types of printer are mainly used with a home PC. They give the user good quality text and graphic output for less than £100. They also allow the user to print in colour on different types of specialised paper such as photographic, envelopes, labels, card and acetates. The cost of replacing the ink can be expensive as the user has to normally buy both black and colour cartridges.

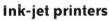

▲ A typical ink-jet printer

An ink–jet printer consists of a print head which contains many nozzles (typically 64). Jets of ink are sprayed from each nozzle onto the paper. A bubble jet printer is an ink–jet printer that operates by heating the ink before spraying it. Sometimes if the printer is not used for a period of time the nozzles on the print head get blocked, which means the user has to use a cleaning head utility program to clear the nozzles.

Laser printers

These printers are used in school networks and offices. They resemble photocopiers in appearance and they produce high quality output of both text and graphics. A reasonable laser printer will print around 20 pages per minute in a quiet fashion. For this to happen laser printers contain their own memory where pages can temporarily be stored before printing. Although laser printers are more expensive to purchase than ink–jet printers they are suitable for large volumes of data. The ink is powder based and is supplied in the form of a toner kit. Laser printers can also print in colour.

Dot matrix printers

Dot Matrix printers are known as impact printers because the print head strikes the paper through an ink ribbon. The print head is made up of a series of pins laid out in rows and columns. Typically a dot matrix printer has 24 pins whereby each character is formed as a pattern of dots. They dots are created by pins striking a ribbon and leaving an image of a character on the page.

They are not as popular due to the development of ink–jet printers but are still used when organisations need to produce carbon copy printouts such as invoices and payslips. The advantage of this is the cheap cost of printing multiple copies of data. Compared to other printers they are cheaper to operate but the quality of output is low. The more pins in the print head, the better the quality of the printout.

Data storage devices

Data storage can be divided into two categories:

- Internal memory (RAM and ROM)
- External memory (Backing storage)

Internal memory is discussed near the beginning of this chapter.

External data storage devices allow programs and data to be stored permanently. Programs and data held on external storage devices must be transferred to the RAM to allow the user to have access.

External storage devices are grouped into categories:

- Magnetic disks
- Optical disks
- Magnetic tape streamers

These devices can be compared in terms of storage capacity, speed of access and retrieval, read and write capability and cost.

■ Floppy disk

Floppy disks are circular, plastic, coated disks with a magnetised surface. The most common floppy disk in use is almost 3.5 inches in diameter. Because they are flexible, they are placed in a 3.5 inch hard rigid plastic sleeve for protection. The storage capacity of a floppy disk is 1.44 MB. Before a floppy disk can be used it must be formatted to allow the floppy disk drive to read and write to and from the surface. This involves a process on mapping out tracks and sectors on the surface by the disk drive to enable data to be stored and later retrieved. Also the formatting process will set up a root directory to allow filenames and their tracks and sector numbers to be stored. Most floppy disk manufacturers sell their floppy disks already formatted for use on a standard PC.

Floppy disks are small and portable and were designed to transfer data from one computer to another. Due to their limited capacity of 1.44 MB they cannot store large graphical files and video images. Although compression software assists in reducing the size of files, floppy disks are best suited for storing text files.

Software such as MS Office would require a lot of floppy disks to store all the programs hence the manufacturer supplies it on a CD–ROM or optical disk.

Their operation involves using a read/write head built into the floppy disk drive to access the data on the floppy disk or write a new file to

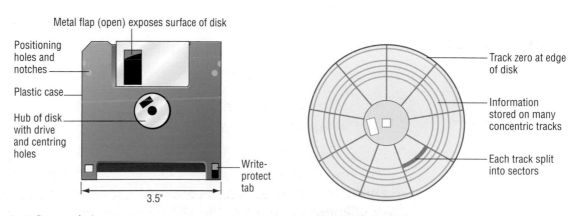

Metal flap (open) exposes surface of disk

Positioning holes and notches

Plastic case

Hub of disk with drive and centring holes

Write-protect tab

3.5"

Track zero at edge of disk

Information stored on many concentric tracks

Each track split into sectors

▲ A floppy disk   ▲ Floppy disk tracks

the floppy disk. They are slow compared to other storage devices. The read/write head in the disk drive makes contact with the surface hence a reduction in the lifespan causing data corruption problems. Another drawback of using floppy disks is that they can easily be damaged.

▲ A Zip drive and disk. Each disk can hold up to 250 MB of data

Special high capacity floppy disks called Zip disks are available to solve the limitations of the capacity of a floppy disk but they require a special drive called a Zip drive. They are slightly larger than floppy discs and can store up to 250 MB of data. The cost of Zip disks has fallen to below £10, but you need to purchase a Zip drive. Apart from the increased capacity of a Zip disk they are more durable than the 3.5 inch floppy disk. They write and read data faster than floppy disk drives but are slower than hard disk drives.

A Jaz drive is even better than a Zip drive. It can store up to 2 GB and is much faster at data transfer than a Zip drive which makes it attractive as backup storage on a standalone PC.

■ Hard disk

▲ Hard drive

The hard drive is the main storage device in most computer systems. A typical hard disk drive consists of a number of rigid disks stacked on top of each other. Each disk has two surfaces. The surfaces of the disks are magnetised hence the name magnetic disk. They are similar to floppy disks as each surface is laid out in tracks and sectors. While a floppy disk drive has only one read/write head, hard disk drives have a read/write head for each surface.

Hard disk drives are contained in sealed units to protect against damage from dirt and dust. The read/write access speeds are much greater than those of a floppy disk.

Compared with a floppy disk they are large in capacity. Typically you would receive an 80 GB capacity hard drive on a standalone PC. The main drawback is that since a hard drive is built into a standard PC it is not portable. Another drawback compared with a floppy disk is that if the hard disk is damaged you will lose a lot more data. Hard disks are mainly used to store the operating system such as Windows XP, applications software such as Microsoft Office and users' datafiles.

■ Optical disks

These type of storage media include:

● CD-ROM
● CD-R
● CD-RW
● DVD

Read-only CDs

These are formally called CD-ROM (Compact Disc-Read Only Memory). In appearance they look like ordinary music CDs. They are purchased with the information already on them and are *read only*. This means no new information can be saved and no existing information can be erased.

Data is burned on to the surface by a laser beam which makes small indentations known as pits. This means the data on the CD cannot be deleted or edited in any way when data is read. Since the data is packed closely together CD-ROMs have a huge capacity compared to magnetic disks. A typical CD-ROM holds up to 650 MB. This makes them suitable for multimedia applications. They are also more reliable and faster to access than floppy disks. They are also used for:

● storing archive material
● encyclopaedias
● distribution of software by software companies.

ALL THESE **WORM** THINGS SEEM TO DO IS READ!

Writeable CDs

These are classified into two types:

■ CD-R (CD Recordable)
■ CD-RW (CD Rewriteable)

The CD-R is a blank CD that can be written to only once but can be read many times. Therefore it is often referred to as a WORM (Write Once, Read Many) disk. CD-RWs can be written to, erased and rewritten many times just like a floppy disk. They are more expensive than CD-R disks and can only be used in a suitable drive which is called a CD-RW drive.

26 CD-ROMs at
650 MB each

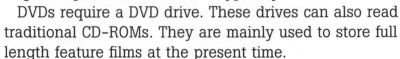

1 DVD at 17 GB

▲ DVD capacity

DVD (Digital Versatile Disk)

These look like ordinary CDs and are mainly used at home as a replacement for video tapes. They are sometimes referred to as DVD-ROM as they were designed to be read only. In more recent times DVD-R has been manufactured which allows for recording onto a DVD. The capacity is huge compared to a CD-ROM, typically 17 GB.

DVDs require a DVD drive. These drives can also read traditional CD-ROMs. They are mainly used to store full length feature films at the present time.

Magnetic tape streamers

These are also referred to as digital audio tapes (DAT). They are similar to magnetic and optical disks in that they store data permanently. Data is stored in blocks and between each block there is a gap on the tape known as the interblock gap.

Magnetic tape works on the principle of *serial access* which means all data before the required item must be read before the required item is accessed.

Magnetic tape can store huge amounts of data cheaply and is suitable as a backup to a hard disk. On a network you will find a magnetic tape streamer attached to the file server. At the end of each school day it is used to backup the hardware as a security measure, in case the hard drive fails.

The magnetic tape streamers use magnetic tape cartridges which can hold around 60 GB of data. At the end of each day an *archive* program is run which will backup all work onto the tape streamer.

▶ Magnetic tape cartridges

10 Information Systems   C2(b)

> ▶ In this section you will learn about data and information.
> ▶ You will also learn how to collect data using well-designed data collection forms and how to ensure that the data collected is valid and accurate.
> ▶ You will examine the advantages and disadvantages associated with data capture techniques.
> ▶ You will look at different file formats and how they can be used.
> ▶ The concept of a relational database and the advantages of storing data in this way will be investigated.
> ▶ You need to learn the definitions of these terms:

- Check digit
- Data
- Field
- File
- Flat files
- Form design
- Format check
- Data collection
- Data compression

- Data integrity
- Data redundancy
- Data security
- Information
- Length check
- Lookup table
- Pixels
- Portability
- Presence check

- Range check
- Record
- Resolution
- Relational database
- Spell check
- Type check
- Validation
- Verification

> ■ You need to expand all of these acronyms:

- ASCII
- csv
- dpi
- gif

- jpeg
- mpeg
- OMR
- OCR

- rtf
- tiff
- pict

Information and data – what is the difference?

> Only candidates taking the full course will study this section.

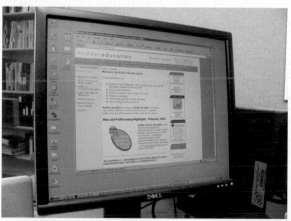

▶ A computer with an information system showing on the screen

An information system, consisting of hardware and software working together, takes data as input and converts it into information.

An information system *processes* the **data** to produce **information**.

▶ Data vs. information

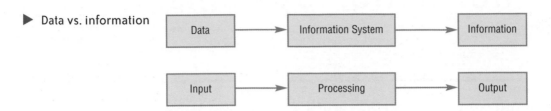

Information and data

| C2(b) Define the difference between data and information. |

Data is raw facts and figures which have not been given a meaning. For example the following list could be described as a set of data:

85, 60, 65, 90, 70, 50, 40, 77, 60

The data can be given a context or meaning. This can be done by describing the data. For example, the following is a list of student marks, as percentages, for this year's French examination:

85%   60%   65%   90%   70%   50%   40%   77%   60%

The data has now become information since it has been given a meaning. Information can also be produced by **processing** the data. Processing the data means to take the values and manipulate them to produce more information.

- What information could be produced by processing this data?
  The average class mark for French could be calculated.
- What is the average mark for this class?
- How can this information be useful to the teacher or her pupils?
- What other information could be produced from the data provided on the sheet?

Teacher Mark Sheet

Subject: French   Class: 9B
Teacher: Mrs Black

Name	Mark (%)
John Jones	85
Mary Smith	60
Anne Cleese	65
Hannah Greer	90
Giles Clarke	70
Alan Gray	50
Mark Black	40
Ellen Roddy	77
Jack Smyth	60

Information is data which has been processed in some way to give it meaning. If the Average Mark for this class is calculated, the data has been processed to give the teacher useful information. ICT systems produce information which has been formatted so that an end user can make good use of it. This information is normally paper based, for example a report, or digital in the case of output which is sent to a computer screen. Before producing information it is necessary to *record the data*. This is known as data capture.

Collecting data

■ Form design

2(b) Discuss features important in form design.

When an organisation or individual wishes to collect data there are some factors to consider. Most of the time a business, school or organisation will use a **form** to collect data. In order that the information is collected effectively, thought must be given to the design of the form. Some questions to be asked by the person designing the form are:

● How will the data be collected?
● Who will provide the data?
● How will the data be used or processed to give information?
● How much data will be collected?

There are a number of ways in which data can be collected.

● Paper based forms.
● Computer based forms.
● Automated data capture.

Paper based forms will be used to collect data from people and then the data will be keyed in to the computer.

Screen based forms are developed to be filled out online or on a computer screen. The advantage of using a screen based form is that data is typed directly and does not have to be transferred from paper. This cuts down on the possibility of human error when entering the data.

In the case of a form it is important to consider the design features. The design quality of the form will have an effect on the data captured. For example if the form is difficult to fill out people will not want to complete it. If the form takes a long time to fill out, some forms may be left incomplete. The quality of the data collected will have an effect on the information produced. Designers should ensure that forms are designed which have clearly presented instructions and sufficient space to enter the required details.

A form should include:

● a title suitable for the purpose of the form
● a logo (if appropriate) representing the company or organisation collecting the data
● a prompt which represents each item of data to be collected
● a suitable space to enter each item of data, the space can be on a line or in the form of a box, tick box, radio button
● suitable instructions, either on or with the form
● suitable text on the purpose of the form.

When designing a form the following should be considered:

● The font chosen should be suitable for the form's intended audience.
● The font should vary in size to emphasise section and headings.

▲ A driving test application form and the instructions.

- Colour should be used to enhance the form where appropriate, for example to break it down into sections.
- Images such as company logos should be included but should not obscure areas of the form.
- Instructions should clearly explain the purpose of the form.

Forms should ask clearly for the data required and should not ask for any more than necessary. The completion of a form should allow users to make selections using tick boxes or radio buttons, this will cut down on incorrect data.

A good form is easily completed and collects the correct data. A form is useless if it collects only part of the required data. This will impact on the quality of the information produced.

Data checking – verification and validation

Tip: Have you ever had to change your password on the computer system? Why do you have to type the new password twice? This is a form of data verification.

When a paper based form is used it is necessary to take the data from the form and enter it into the computer. When this happens we must ensure that the data entered from the paper based form is correct and accurate. A computer operator will enter the data from the form. It is important that mistyped data is detected by the computer system. In order to detect this type of error, **verification** of the data input is performed.

Data verification is carried out to ensure that data keyed into a computer has been accurately transferred from a paper based form. The most common way of performing verification is to key the data twice. Data is keyed into the computer system twice by two different computer operators and then the computer system compares the two sets of data. Any mismatched data is rejected. Any rejected data is re-entered. This ensures that data is transferred accurately and correctly. Another method of verification is proofreading. Documents once typed can be proofread to ensure that they contain correct and accurate information.

■ Using computer based forms

It is common nowadays to collect data directly using a computer based form. This means that the data is keyed into the computer directly with no paper based form being completed. An example of this can be seen when you visit a travel agent to book a holiday. All of the holiday data is entered directly onto a computer based form.

▲ A travel agent completes a holiday request using a computer based form.

The holiday booking request is then processed to see if the holiday requested is available.

Data collected using a data entry screen must be checked, by the software, before it is accepted by the computer system. Checking data to ensure that it is acceptable and sensible is called validation. **Validation** of data ensures that the data is present, of the correct type, in the correct range and of the correct length. These checks can be made on data to be entered into the system. A validation check is made automatically by the system and an error message is displayed if data is incorrect. There are a number of different types of validation checks.

Presence check

A presence check will ensure that data has been entered into an area on the form. This check means that data which must be entered is not omitted. You can see examples of this type of check when you fill out an onscreen form. Onscreen forms are used:

- on websites – when you register on a website or buy products online, such fields often have a red asterisk beside them.

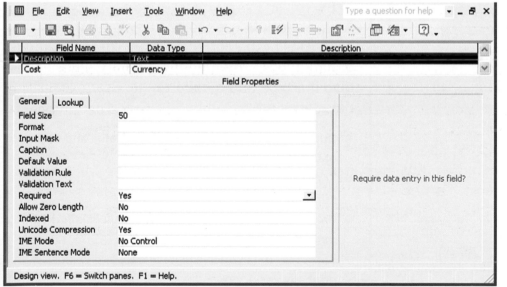

- for entering data onto an onscreen form for use in an ICT system. This is common in database applications.

The design view of a database table shows that a **presence** check will be carried out for the field *Description,* because Required is set to Yes. This is sensible because we would not want to enter a new product without giving a description for it.

The next screen shot shows the error message that will be displayed if a user tries to enter a product ID without entering the description for it.

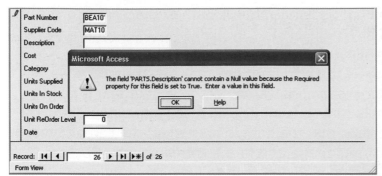

Length

A length check will ensure that data entered is of the correct length. For example the Part Number in the above database may have a length check to ensure that it is six characters long.

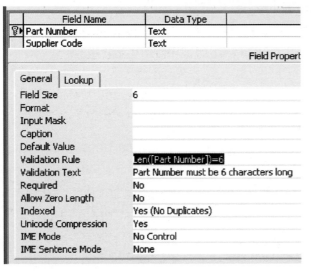

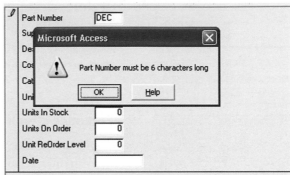

Type

A type check is used to ensure that the data entered is of the correct format. There is a range of data types. When defining data we usually give it a type and a valid range. Examples of data types are:

- Numeric – data takes on a numeric value and such data can be used in calculations.
- Text – data can be made up of letters or letters and numbers.
- Date – Data takes on a value which is formatted as a date.
- Boolean – Data which can have only two values, normally yes or no.

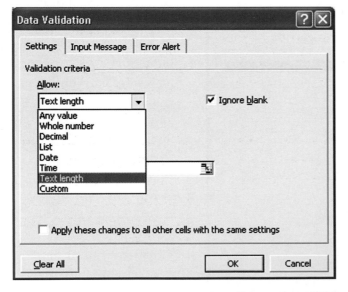

- Currency – data which represents money values.

Type checks can be implemented in a variety of ways. Some spreadsheet applications allow cells to be validated by allowing only certain data types to be entered. Below we can see some of the different data type checks which can be made on data entered.

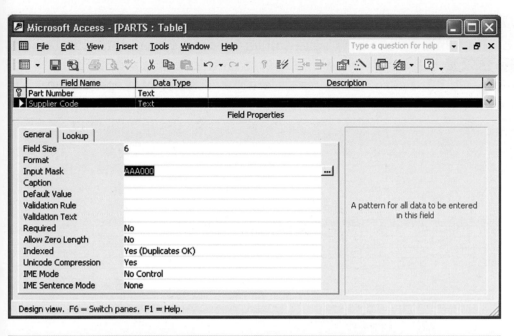

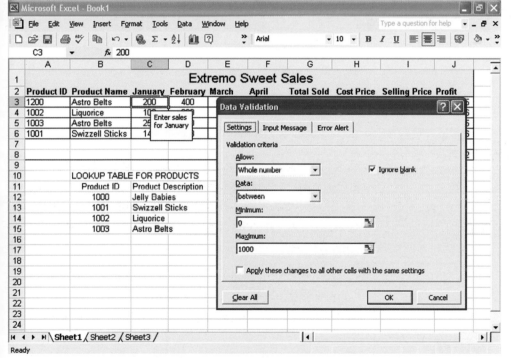

Format

Some database packages allow the user to specify exactly what format the data being entered should take. In the example, the field Supplier Code is assigned an Input Mask, which requires that three letters followed by three numbers are entered. The database will not allow data to be entered in any other format.

Range

A range check ensures that data entered is within a given range. For example:

- Customer number can take on values between 1 and 500.
- Student grades can take on values between "A" and "E".

This data validation has set a range check to ensure that values entered into cell C3 are in the correct range, that is 0–1000.

Lookup tables

Lookup tables or lists hold valid values for data. When data is entered the lookup table is checked to ensure that the data is within the allowable list. These can be used very successfully in a spreadsheet application.

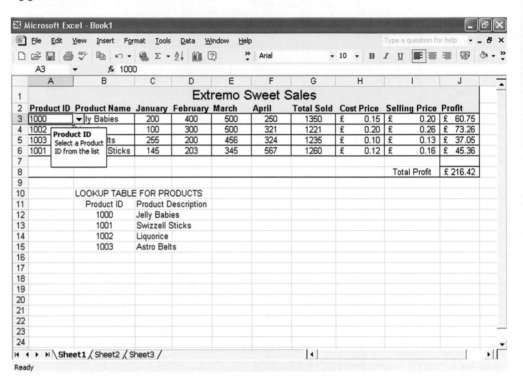

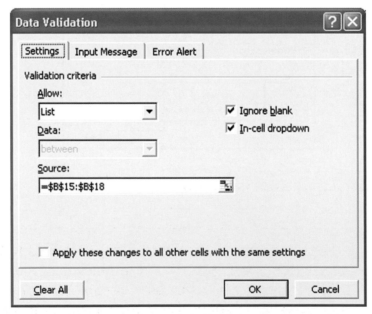

Here you can see that cell A3 has been validated so that only values in the lookup table can be selected. The resulting error message comes from the data validation set in the box below. The lookup values are located in cells B15 to B18.

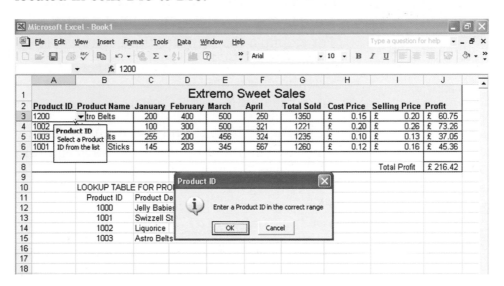

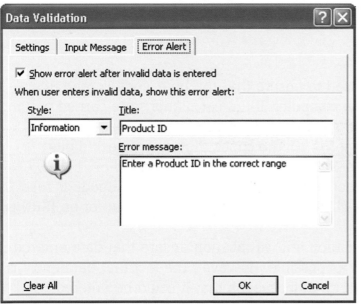

This form of validation ensures that only values in the lookup table are acceptable. Another point to note is that the Product Name will automatically appear.

Check digit

Cross reference with section on EPOS.

Check digits are characters which are added to the end of a code. The check digit is compared with the results of a calculation using the code. If the results of the calculation do not match the check digit, the code has to be input again. They are commonly found on ISBN numbers in books. They are also found at the end of the Universal Product Code (UPC) or barcode on items in supermarkets.

▲ An ISBN on a barcode

Calculate the check digit for this book.

■ Working out a check digit

ISBN is the abbreviation for the International Standard Book Number. ISBN numbers are 10 digits in length. An ISBN takes the form X-XX-XXXXXX-X.

Here is a sample barcode with the ISBN displayed below it.

For example the ISBN for the book *History for CCEA GCSE* is 0-340-86919-4

4 is the check digit.

To calculate the check digit:

1 Take the ISBN code and weight each digit.
2 Then we multiply the digit by the weighting.

Weighting	10	9	8	7	6	5	4	3	2
ISBN	0	3	4	0	8	6	9	1	9
Result	0	27	32	0	48	30	36	3	18

The results of multiplication are added together:
0 + 27 + 32 + 0 + 48 + 30 + 36 + 3 + 18 = 194

3 Now divide 194 by 11. = 17 remainder 7.
4 Take the remainder from 11.

11 − 7 = 4

4 is the check digit used to ensure that the book code is read or entered correctly at the computer. If the calculations are carried out and the result obtained is not equal to the check digit the code will be rejected. If the remainder is 10, the check digit is X. Check digits provide another form of validating data.

Barcodes also use check digits. In a supermarket a barcode is read from an item and a calculation similar to that carried out for an ISBN is carried out.

The methods of validation and verification ensure that data entered is as correct and reliable as possible. However, the fact that data entry is carried out by a human operator means that it could be entered erroneously, even if it is valid. Operators can enter data incorrectly.

Some software packages have validation features built in. We can validate data when it is entered into a computer system. Consider the use of a word processor. How is the data entered validated or checked? The spell checker can be used to check accuracy and to report on any spelling inconsistencies. The spell checker is limited in what it can detect as inaccuracies.

● Can you think of any examples?

Data capture

● How can we cut down on human error?

Another method of entering data into a computer is by direct data capture. This is when the data is not entered or typed in by an operator, but is read directly into the computer using a special method and readers. Two methods of data capture are:

■ OMR – Optical Mark Recognition

This method of data capture scans forms which have been filled in using marks or ticks. The documents have empty boxes printed onto them. OMR uses light to detect the position of marks on paper. The marks on the paper must be placed accurately to ensure that the data being input is read accurately. The OMR technology converts information about the presence or absence of marks into digital data. It enables high speed reading of large quantities of data by the computer without using the keyboard. The OMR reader scans the form, detects the presence of marks and passes the information to the computer for processing by applications software.

OMR is used for the National Lottery. Players of the lottery fill out their number choices onto a paper which has preprinted boxes to select the numbers. The document is then scanned using an optical scanner. The data is read from the paper and a ticket is produced which has the numbers selected printed onto it. This acts as a receipt and is used by players to check off their numbers to see if they match with the winning numbers.

OMR is also used on answer sheets for multiple choice tests. This means the tests can be marked automatically using the OMR scanner. In some schools pupil attendance is recorded on OMR sheets. At the end of each session (morning and afternoon) the attendance sheet is read using the OMR reader and pupil attendance is recorded.

Advantages of using OMR

● Fast – Inputting large amounts of data can be done quickly as OMR allows many documents to be processed one after the other. The data on the document does not have to be typed; it is read directly by the optical mark reader.
● Accurate – because data is read directly from the document, it eliminates the possibility of typing errors made by humans.
● Data input to a computer using OMR can be analysed to produce high quality information quickly.
● Staff will need minimum training in system use as documents are simply passed into a scanner.

Disadvantages of using OMR

- The cost of buying OMR equipment could be high.
- Documents used must be kept in good condition. The system may not be able to read creased documents.
- OMR input is paper based. The cost of producing specially design forms could be high.
- Unless the forms are recycled after input, it may not be the most environmentally friendly solution.

▶ An OMR form

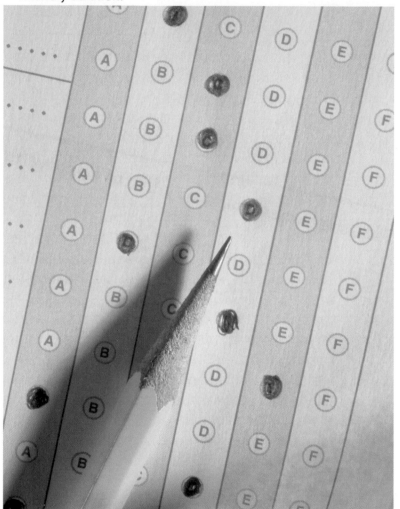

■ OCR – Optical Character Recognition

This is the method used to take paper based documents and transform them into editable computer files. Let us say you need a digital replica of a document like a magazine page, newspaper, fax, or printer output. You may try to retype a document from scratch, but this could take a long time. OCR provides the best alternative to manual typing. This technology makes use of an optical scanner.

Optical scanners will scan any page as a picture. Most scanners have an OCR program included with them. An OCR program can look at the *picture* of the document, *read* the document, and convert it to text. This text is editable in a word processor. When a document is scanned using the OCR facility it is saved as an rtf (rich text file).

Where a high level of accuracy is required, or where a scanner is required to tell the difference between images and text, complex software and specialised hardware is required.

OCR is being used by libraries to digitise and preserve old documents and books. OCR is also used to sort the mail. Millions of letters are sorted every day by OCR machines, considerably speeding up mail delivery. Royal Mail use the postcode to help sort mail.

BT31 2YZ	✓ correct segregation of characters
BT31 2YZ	✗ unable to segregate characters - could be misread as BB1 2YZ
BT31 2YZ	✗ T overlapping character space of 3 - unable to seperate characters

▲ A postcode which is readable by an OCR device with Royal Mail.

▲ Flat bed scanners can be used to scan a paper version of a document.

Advantages of using OCR

- Large quantities of text can be input to the computer quickly.
- An electronic copy of a paper based document can be created without re-typing it.
- Handwriting can be read directly by the computer.

Disadvantages of using OCR

- Documents which are dirty or marked will not be read accurately.
- Systems which are highly accurate are expensive.
- OCR systems will not produce accurate results when required to scan forms (especially with boxes and check boxes), very small text , shady photocopies, mathematical formulae or some handwritten text.

Data structure

■ Flat files

Data stored on an ICT system is stored and organised in **files**. When the data is organised in rows and columns with data values being repeated, it is called a flat file. A flat file looks like a spreadsheet; it is two dimensional and has no related files (or tables). Flat files are easy to create and use. Data is often repeated in a flat file and therefore they can be quite large in size. This means that the computer has more data to read through, so accessing and searching through them can be slow. A flat file could be described as a file containing text or data separated by commas or tabs, such as a csv file (see page 156).

Files are made up of **records** and each record is made up of a set of **fields**. In a file a row usually represents a record and a set of field values are contained in a column.

Data fields

Fields can hold different types of data. The data type tell us whether the data is:

- Numeric
- Text
- Boolean
- Date
- Currency

See section on Validation for definitions.

Records

A record is a unit of data which is made up of a number of fields. There is one record per item in the database.

Look at this spreadsheet. The structure of the spreadsheet could be described as a flat file.

	A	B	C	D	E	F	G
1	**Pupil ID**	**Surname**	**Forename**	**Subject**	**Coursework**	**Examination**	**Total**
2	1000	**Black**	Anne	French	30	45	75
3	1050	**Doherty**	Elaine	Spanish	45	48	93
4	1060	**Matthews**	Richard	Spanish	33	40	73
5	1000	**Black**	Anne	German	44	45	89

- Can you identify records and fields in this file?

There are **four records** and each record is made up of **six fields**.

The field names are Pupil ID, Surname, Forename, Subject, Coursework, Examination, Total.

The data types for each field are:

Field Name	Data Type
Pupil ID	Numeric
Surname	Text
Forename	Text
Subject	Text
Coursework	Numeric
Examination	Numeric
Total	Numeric

Redundancy

This file has a very simple row and column structure. There are no relationships between data. The main weakness of this type of file is that data has to be repeated. Look at the entry for "Anne Black". Her name is recorded twice because she studies two languages. In a relational database system, this would not happen. The surname and forename of each person would be stored only once and a related table would be created to hold the rest of the data. The two tables would then be linked. When data is repeated unnecessarily it is said to be **redundant**. If another entry is made for Anne Black the file would now look like this:

	A	B	C	D	E	F	G
1	**Pupil ID**	**Surname**	**Forename**	**Subject**	**Coursework**	**Examination**	**Total**
2	1000	**Black**	Anne	*French*	30	45	75
3	1050	**Doherty**	Elaine	*Spanish*	45	48	93
4	1060	**Matthews**	Richard	*Spanish*	33	40	73
5	1000	**Black**	Anne	*German*	44	45	89
6	1000	**Black**	Annie	*Spanish*	33	44	77

The new entry contains data which is not correct. Anne Black's forename has been recorded as "Annie".

Integrity

The more often data has to be recorded the higher the possibility of the data having an error or inconsistency. The user of the data must be able to rely on the correctness and accuracy of the data. The correctness, reliability and accuracy of the data is called **data integrity**.

■ Relational databases

A relational database holds information in files or tables which are linked together using relationships between fields in the tables. The data is organised in a way which makes searching and sorting easy.

The relationships between the tables means that data is less likely to be repeated so there is *less* data redundancy. The number of times that data has to be re-typed is kept to a minimum so data is more likely to be free from typing errors. This means that the *integrity* of the data is likely to be better.

Key field

Each table in a relational database has a field which is called a **key field**. The key field is a value which will uniquely identify each record in the table. It can be of any data type. In the case of the pupil, the unique key field would be the Pupil ID.

Relationships

Relationships are links that have been made between two tables. The links are made using fields that are contained within both tables.

▶ Linking tables in a relational database

From the flat files example above, the following tables could be created:

One PUPIL has *many* MARKS. This means that there is a one-to-many relationship between the two tables.

We can use a relational database package such as Microsoft Access to create the relationships between the tables. The two tables are linked

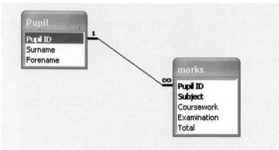

▲ A one-to-many relationship created between two tables in Microsoft Access.

on Pupil ID, as this field occurs in both tables. Each Pupil ID entered into the Marks table must be present in the Pupil table. The database will not allow a mark to be entered for a pupil who is not in the Pupil table. This helps ensure the integrity of the data.

When the tables are created and the data is entered, each pupil's name is entered only once regardless of the number of results that have been recorded for that pupil.

▶ Pupil data recorded in a Microsoft Access database

Pupil ID	Surname	Forename	
1000 Black	Anne		

Subject	Coursework	Examination	Total
French	30	45	75
German	44	45	89
Spanish	33	44	77

Pupil ID	Surname	Forename	
1050 Doherty	Elaine		

Subject	Coursework	Examination	Total
Spanish	45	48	43

Pupil ID	Surname	Forename	
1060 Matthews	Richard		

Subject	Coursework	Examination	Total
Spanish	33	40	73

Data Security

Cross reference with the Data Protection Act.

It is important when data is stored about people that it is kept secure. When you study the Data Protection Act (see page 231) you will see that people who store and use data have the responsibility of keeping it secure.

A relational database stores data in many tables in one single database in one location. Relational databases can allow many people to access the data at once. Data must be kept secure so that there is no unauthorised access to it. It is easier to keep the data secure in a relational database because only one copy of the data is held. In most databases there is a software which manages access to the database. Different users will be given different access privileges. For example in the case of the Pupil–Mark database, a pupil may be able to view his/her marks but may not be able to change them. Some access privileges provided by a database are:

- Read only – allows the user to look at the data in the table, but not to change it.
- Read/Write – allows the user to look at the data and also to change it.
- Read/Write/Delete – allows the user to look at the data, change data and delete records.

The system administrator can give different users different access privileges. These features of a relational database mean that data security can be easily maintained.

A relational database is better than a flat file system because:

- the security of data stored in a single location can be managed more easily
- different access privileges can be given to users so that the data can be protected from unauthorised access
- repetition of data is kept to a minimum so there is little or no data redundancy
- files can be searched more quickly because there is very little repeated data
- most data is recorded only once and so it will be correct, accurate and reliable throughout the database
- the use of key fields and relationships allow the database to ensure the integrity of the data
- relationships between files means that data from many tables in the database can be searched at once.

Data portability

Data portability is the ability to transfer data from one system or software application to another without having to re-enter the data. The format in which data is held will indicate whether or not that data is portable between different software applications and different computer systems.

■ Comma Separated Variable (csv) files

A csv file can be created using Microsoft Notepad or Microsoft Word. The file created below contains three fields separated by commas. The field names are entered first. Each record in the file is on a new line.

```
Date,Time,Temperature
12/12/02,2pm,12
12/12/02,2:30pm,10
12/12/02,3pm,15
12/12/02,3:30pm,19
12/12/02,4pm,9
```

The file has been saved as *Temp.csv*. This file can then be opened using a spreadsheet. The contents will appear as follows:

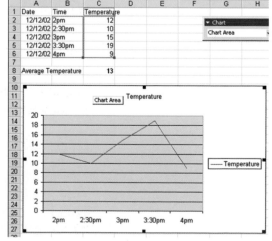

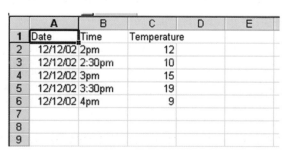

Once the data is available in the spreadsheet, it can be manipulated and graphs can be drawn. Save the spreadsheet as **temp.xls**.

The contents of *temp.xls* can be imported into the database. CSV files are produced from data logging equipment.

● Can you see how we can take the data produced and import it easily into an application which can convert data to information?

This is a simple example of data portability. The csv file format allows the data to be used in a word processor, a database and a spreadsheet.

■ File formats

The format in which a file is stored will determine the portability of the file. Files can be made up of text or graphics. Each type of file can be stored using different formats.

CSV files – Comma Separated Variables

Files of this format hold data which is separated by commas. In general a comma separates a field value and a single line in the file normally represents a record. CSV files can be imported directly to spreadsheets or databases as rows and columns.

RTF – Rich Text Format

This file format allows users to transfer data between different applications. For example a user using Word 2000 could save a file as rtf and send it to a user who uses a different word processor. Documents scanned using the OCR facility of a scanner are usually saved as rtf documents. This means that the document can be opened using a variety of word-processing applications.

JPEG – Joint Photographic Experts Group

This format is any graphic image file produced by using a jpeg standard. This group of experts develops standards for compressing images. Jpegs are commonly used on webpages and are normally small files. If a file is stored as a jpeg it can be used in any document in a number of different operating systems. For example jpegs can be opened in the Windows and Apple Macintosh operating systems. This makes them highly portable.

MPEG – Moving Picture Experts Group

This format is any moving picture produced by using a MPEG standard. This group of experts develops standards for compressing digital video. This is a compressed file format.

PICT

PICT files are the Macintosh native picture format. PICT files are used by Macintosh graphics applications, they can support high quality images and can be compressed.

TIFF – Tagged Image File Format

This is a graphics file format and stores bitmapped images. Graphics can be black and white, grey-scale or coloured. This file format is portable between different applications and types of computers. It can be used in a Windows and Apple Macintosh environment.

GIF – Graphic Interchange Format

This graphics file format supports compressed images. They are usually small in size and are suitable for inclusion on webpages. Colour quality can be a problem.

TXT – Text file

This is a simple text file which will hold letters and numbers but not formats such as bold and italic.

ASCII – American Standard Code for Information Interchange

An ASCII file is a plain text file that can be read with a simple Windows Notepad program or any text editor. You can look at an ASCII file using the Windows Notepad or WordPad programs, but if the file is saved after viewing it these programs may alter the file characteristics. The same file viewed in Notepad and Wordpad may look different. Notepad shows text with bolder and larger characters and cannot show page breaks. WordPad shows an ASCII file with its default font, which is smaller, and can show page breaks. ASCII files can be imported into a word processor but the ASCII file may not appear in its original format. Each word processor will apply its own page layouts to ASCII files. ASCII files are highly portable and are supported by almost every application.

MIDI – Musical Instrument Digital Interface

These files are produced when digital musical instruments are connected as input devices to the computer. They are sound files (see page 223).

MP3

MP3 music files are CD quality compressed recordings that are about ten times smaller than the equivalent CD WAV/AIFF file. MP3s are reduced in size by filtering out all noise that is not detectable to the human ear.

Data compression

Data transmission and storage costs money. Digital data is not always stored in its most compact form. It is stored in an easy to use form which is generally larger than is actually needed to represent the information. Data compression is used to convert digital data to as small a size as possible without losing any of the information contained in a file.

■ Why compress data?

When we transmit images over the World Wide Web it is important that they can be downloaded in an acceptable time. If we need to download a high quality coloured picture over a 56 kbps modem it will be quicker if it has been compressed. A TIFF file of 600 kB when converted to a gif file will contain approximately 300 kB of data. The same TIFF file converted to a jpeg will contain about 50 kB of data. Download time will be reduced significantly if we choose the gif or jpeg format of compression.

Bitmapped graphics

Graphic compression can be done using a graphics package. The graphic can be saved using the specified format to a given resolution.

Bitmap graphics depend on resolution for quality. The resolution of a graphic is the number of pixels used to represent the image. A pixel is the smallest unit drawable on a graphic. Graphics are made up of a grid of pixels. The more pixels in the grid, the higher the resolution of the graphic. This will make the graphic bigger in size and of better quality. Bitmaps are better for photographs. They cannot be stretched without losing image quality.

Bitmap graphics can be compressed or saved in other file formats for example gif or jpeg to reduce their size.

Vector graphics

Not all graphics are dependent on their resolution for clarity. Vector graphics are formed from vector objects, like the lines on a *join the dots* image. They can be stretched or shrunk without losing the quality of their image. Vector graphics do not depend on resolution for quality. This means that no matter how many dots per inch you're using on screen or in print, your image will look the same. Because of their structure they can generally be saved as smaller files than bitmaps.

▲ a) Graphic image which has not used enough pixels
b) The same graphic at a higher resolution

■ Data compression tools

Tools to compress data are available. WinZip will compress files to a fraction of their size. Files which have been compressed in this way are called ZIP files. These files are compressed before being transported and must then be uncompressed at their destination before they can be used.

Data compression tools can also compress full folders of information and store them as a single file for emailing or transporting. The destination computer must have the data compression tool so that the ZIP file can be extracted.

Data compression tools are useful:

- when a user wants to email a large file
- to reduce the time taken to transmit an email
- when a file is slightly larger than the size of a floppy disk, the compression tools can make the file smaller so it will fit on the disk
- to save storage space.

Many different types of data can be compressed using the correct file format:

- Graphics can be compressed using jpeg or gif format.
- Music files can be compressed using MP3 format.
- Video files can be compressed using mpeg format.

In all cases the purpose of compression is to make the files smaller in size to give efficient digital transmission or storage of the data.

11 Digital Communication Systems

▶ In this section you will learn about how computers are linked together to form networks. You will see that networks can exist in a single building or over a large geographic area and study the ways in which networks are kept secure.

▶ You will learn about the Internet, how data is transferred along communications lines and the equipment required to use the Internet.

▶ Networks allow many types of digital communication. You will learn about some ways of communicating across a network.

▶ You need to learn the definitions of these terms:

- Access
- Backup
- Bandwidth
- Browser
- Digital camera
- Electronic mail
- Encryption

- Facsimile
- File server
- Internet
- Internet Service Provider (ISP)
- Intranet
- Password
- Protocol

- Router
- Search engine
- Teleconferencing
- Topology
- Wireless technology
- World Wide Web

■ You need to expand all of these acronyms:

- LAN
- WAN
- WWW
- ISP

- HTML
- URL
- ISDN
- PSTN

- ADSL
- PC

Data networks – LANs and WANs

A network consists of a set of computers which are linked together. Computers which are linked together can share resources like printers and software communicating with each other.

Networks can be made up of a few computers linked together on a single site in a Local Area Network (LAN) or they can be linked via powerful computers over a large geographic area in a Wide Area Network (WAN). The Internet is a WAN.

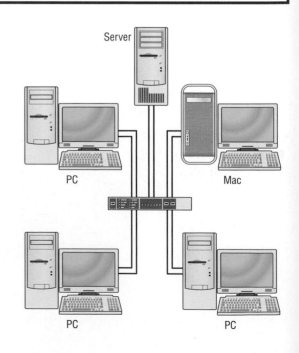

▶ A network schematic

Local Area Networks – LANs

This type of network is used in places like schools and offices. It is spread over a small geographic area such as one or two buildings. The network links computers in the buildings together using network cables. The data is transmitted from one computer to another along the network cables. Computers on a LAN can be networked in a variety of ways.

Computer networks are constructed using a combination of the following components:

■ File server

A file server is the main computer on the network. It is more powerful than all of the other computers, with a large amount of RAM and hard disk space. It will hold:

- the network operating system software such as Microsoft Windows XP
- application software such as Microsoft Word
- user files created by the users on the system
- system software which will manage the network resources and security
- utility software such as a virus checker.

The file server manages communication across the network and makes sure that only authorised users log on to the system.

The log on process is done by making use of **usernames**, **passwords** and **access codes**.

▶ A typical network card.

■ Network interface card

Each computer must have a network card so that it can communicate with the file server and all other computers on the network.

■ Network cables

The **network cables** plug into the back of each computer and link the computers together. These cables plug directly into the network card contained inside each computer. You can ask your teacher to show you the back of a computer which is linked to your school network.

▶ A typical data cable with RJ-45 connector.

▶ A system switch

■ Switches

A switch is a single connection point for a group of computers. The switch allows many computers to be connected to it directly using network cables. The switch is connected to the file server and organises communication between the file server and the computers connected to it. Not all networks use switches.

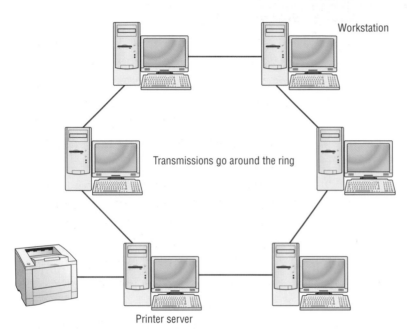

Workstation

Transmissions go around the ring

Printer server

▲ A ring network

■ Network software

When a computer is part of a network, the network software must be installed on it. This allows it to communicate with the file server and other computers.

■ Network topology

Networks can be set up in different shapes. This is called the **topology** of the network. There are three main topologies:

- ■ Ring Network
- ■ Bus Network
- ■ Star Network

Ring network

In a ring network all of the computers are linked together in the shape of a ring. Data travels around the network in one direction, between the computers. If a computer in the ring breaks down or is switched off the network will not be able to operate. If a cable becomes damaged or broken the network will not work. This type of network uses less cabling and so may be cheaper to set up. There is no file server. In this case the network is connected *peer-to-peer*. This means that each computer is connected to the next and they can 'see' each other's hard disks.

Bus network

Bus networks link computers or workstations together using one main cable, called the backbone cable. This cable runs along the network in a single line. Each computer is linked to the main cable. Initial setup of this type of network is easy. The amount of cabling required is less than that needed for a star network and so it is also cheaper to set up.

The main computer or **file server** is placed at one end of the line. If there is a break in the backbone cable, data will not be transmitted to any of the machines. However, if a machine is unplugged or breaks down, the network will continue to function unlike the ring network.

Star network

Star networks have a central file server and all of the computers are linked via a cable to the main computer. A cable is connected between each computer and a switch or hub. The switch or hub is then connected to the main computer via a cable. Groups of computers are clustered together and connected to one hub. This type of network uses a lot of cabling and so is expensive to implement. Communication with the server is faster because each machine has got its own link directly to the server. If one computer on the network breaks down, the network is not affected. All other computers continue to function. If the file server breaks down the entire network will not work. If a hub or switch becomes damaged, the computers connected to it will not communicate over the network.

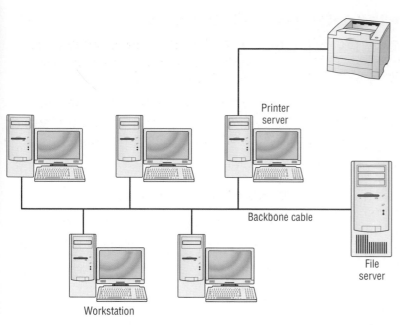

Printer server

Backbone cable

File server

Workstation

▲ A bus network

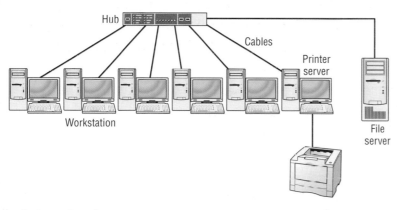

Hub

Cables

Printer server

File server

Workstation

▲ A star network

The advantages of networked computers are:

- Expensive peripherals can be shared between a number of computers. For example one laser printer, one fax or one scanner can be used by several computers in a room or building.
- A single copy of the software is stored on the file server and this is shared by all the computers on the network.
- Users can communicate with each other. This can be done using email or conferencing on the network.
- Users can share files and work on joint projects using shared resources on the network.
- Users have flexible access. They can log on at any computer and accesss their files.

■ Why secure the network?

The network must be protected from:

● unauthorised access by users or hackers
● viruses
● authorised users who might damage important files
● unexpected breakdown resulting in the loss of data
● physical damage.

The network must protect:

● user data
● the software on the file server
● the resources which are shared by users.

■ How is the network kept secure?

Usernames and passwords

Each user on the network is given a unique user name. The user can decide on a password which only they will know. When a user wants to use the network they must log on. Logging on involves entering the username and the password.

The username can be seen but the password appears in asterisk or dot format. When the user clicks on the log on button, software on the file server checks to see if a username with the password entered exists. If the password and username do not match, the person will not be allowed access to the network. This is one way of stopping unauthorised users from getting onto the network. Some networks only allow users a limited number of attempts at logging on and disable the user account for a period of time after unsuccessful log on attempts.

Access levels

Another way of keeping the network secure is to limit the things which users can do on the network. This is done by giving users different **access rights**. For example in a school, pupils, teachers and the system manager have different levels of access.

The log on information opposite shows that a member of staff is currently logged on and that the person has advanced access rights.

A pupil can:

● access software
● use the Internet
● change the content and location of their user files
● change their password
● select a printer to print work.

A teacher can do everything that a pupil can and also:

- give students printer credits
- reset their passwords.

The system manager can do everything a teacher and pupil can do and also:

- set up new users
- delete users
- change the amount of disk storage space that each user is allocated
- copy files between users
- allocate network resources like printers.

This form of access is called tiered access. Each group of users has a different level of access. This protects the network from damage by users.

A file server will also have virus protection software installed. This will protect the network and the computers on it from virus infection. The virus protection software on most networks will be automatically updated at least daily to take account of any new viruses. Viruses can enter the network in a many ways. For example:

- from a floppy disk or other portable storage device
- through the Internet
- by email.

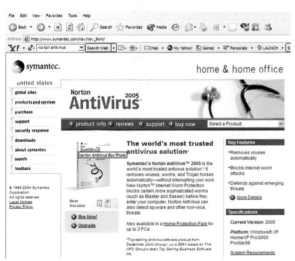

Virus protection software is installed on the file server so that the network is protected from any new viruses. On a network the virus protection software will scan all of the linked PCs each day to ensure that there are no infections. When a user puts a disk or USB bar into the computer it is automatically scanned to make sure it is virus free. If the device contains a virus the user will be notified and the systems administrator will be told also.

■ Data backup on a LAN

User data on the LAN must also be protected. If data is lost the system must have some method of recovering the data. Most network systems use a backup process to make sure that there is a copy of the data that can be loaded on to the system if the original data is lost.

Backup copies of data are stored on magnetic tape. A tape drive is fitted on the file server and a backup of the system is taken at regular intervals. In schools and offices a backup is usually taken every day using a different tape. A backup activity may slow the network down as it uses system resources. Backup is done regularly, when the computer system is not busy, for example during the night. Tapes may be kept for up to 30 days before being reused.

■ Data backup on a PC

Users of standalone PCs should also keep regular backups of data files. This prevents accidental loss of data or software. Windows XP has a special utility which makes it easy for users to back up data.

Users are prompted using a wizard and guided through the steps to the backup of their data.

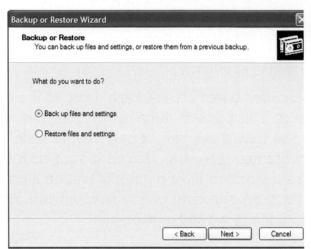
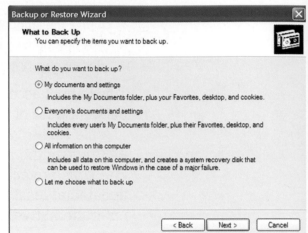

Backups can be made to the existing hard disk or to a removable storage medium with suitable capacity, such as CD-ROM or DVD.

Wide Area Networks – WANs

■ Encryption

Data transmitted across a WAN or a LAN could be intercepted by unauthorised users. To prevent data being intercepted and read during transmission it can be encrypted. Encryption is the process of encoding data which is to be sent across a network, making that data unreadable to anyone who intercepts it. Only a user with the encryption key software can read the data when it arrives at its destination. This is another way of keeping data secure whilst it is travelling on the network.

Businesses and other organisations need to access information on external computer systems. For example, a company which has several branches may want to network the branches so that computers in one branch can talk to computers at another branch. The network would be spread over a large geographic area and is called a WAN – Wide Area Network. The Internet is the biggest WAN in existence. It links many LANs together allowing the users to communicate with each other.

> A router is a piece of hardware which connects a LAN to the Internet.

In Northern Ireland all post-primary schools are linked together on a WAN. If there is a problem with a computer a technician in Belfast can check the machine remotely. The WAN will allow all post-primary schools to communicate with each other.

If LANs are to be connected to the Internet or to WANs special equipment is needed. A router is a device that will translate information from the Internet so that the computers on a LAN can understand it. It will also translate information coming from the LAN to the Internet. A router is an intelligent translator, it will find the shortest route to send data across the network.

Let us look at the structure of a WAN.

A WAN is a collection of networks connected using a telecommunications link. Most WANs make use of the PSTN.

The PSTN – Public Service Telephone Network is the main telecommunications network in the UK. This network was made up of analogue telephones and landlines. Now the PSTN includes many digital features. On this network there are a variety of line types. The connection types have different bandwidths.

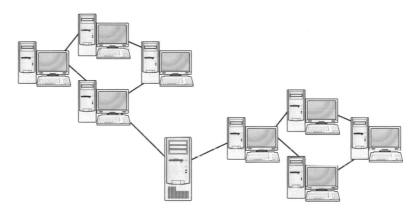

▲ WANs can provide Internet access as well as access to other LANs which can be located anywhere geographically.

■ The main differences between a LAN and a WAN

LAN – Local Area Network	WAN – Wide Area Network
Spread over a small geographic area, usually one or two buildings.	Spread over a vast geographic area throughout countries or the world.
Computers on a LAN can be linked together using copper cabling.	A WAN is a network of networks. The link between networks cannot be copper as data can only travel a short distance on a copper wire. It can be fibre optic, or a wireless link like satellite.

Co

MODEM

YOUR

▲ C
Inter

Mobile phones

▲ A modern mobile phone

The mobile phone uses radio frequency to transmit data. Its size means that it can be carried around easily and used anywhere that there is network coverage. This mobile communication tool means that people can be contacted 24/7. The mobile phone is a highly personal device and many families now have a number of mobile phones in the home.

■ Using a mobile phone to access the Internet

WAP enabled mobile phones can be used to access the Internet. WAP is Wireless Applications Protocol and was designed to allow handheld devices access to the Internet.

WAP is a communication protocol and it is used to access network services and information using mobile devices. Mobile phones use micro-browsers to display information. A micro-browser makes very little demand on the hardware. WAP phones can be used to:

▶ A WAP menu

- view train timetables
- view traffic information
- check weather conditions
- send and receive email
- look up sports results.

▲ A PDA

Handheld devices such as Personal Digital Assistants (PDAs) are also WAP enabled and can be used to access the Internet. One of the most up-to-date handheld devices is the Blackberry. This device allows users to access email and even download attachments as well as being a phone.

■ Short Message Service – SMS

Communication using a mobile phone can be made via a voice telephone call or by using SMS – Short Message Service. This is the text message facility associated with a mobile phone. Users can send messages to other mobile phones on any network. This is done almost instantly. A text message can get through even while a call is in progress. A text message goes to a central message centre and it is forwarded as soon as a transmission space is available. Many mobile phones can now be used to take digital photographs or short movies. These can also be sent to other mobile phones through the message

▶ Mobile phone SMS screen

centre. The message function can also be used to send emails and fax messages.

Email can be sent by SMS through a gateway. The gateway converts the SMS to email format and the provider will forward the email to the recipient.

Mobile phones can *roam*. This means that they can send and receive data and telephone calls whilst in another country. This is useful if people are away from work or home. They will be kept up to date on all current information.

Voice mail enables callers to leave a message if the owner of the telephone is not available or is on another call. This means that no calls will be missed.

Digital image systems

■ Digital television and analogue television

▶ A digital receiver converts digital signals to analogue signals for display on a TV.

Conventional television is transmitted using analogue signals. Digital signals are used to transmit digital TV channels. The digital signal has to be decoded so that a normal TV shows the images and sounds. This is done by using a decoding box, usually supplied from the digital TV provider, for example Sky, or by using a digital television. A digital television has the necessary internal components for converting digital signals to images and sounds.

Digital TV has a number of advantages over analogue TV.

● Digital TV signals can be compressed easier than analogue signals therefore the amount of data which can be sent on a digital signal is much greater.
● Digital communications lines can transmit and receive data; therefore digital TV can be interactive.
● Analogue television can suffer interference. Digital television is less affected by interference, so the digital channel will provide a sharper, clearer picture.

▶ Digital TV can provide sharper and clearer pictures

a) Analogue TV   b) Digital TV

● Digital television pictures are broadcast in widescreen format, just like at the movies and on DVDs.

▶ Widescreen format

● Digital television outputs high quality stereo sound using MPEG technology.
● More channels are available on digital TV because of the larger bandwidth available.
● Digital television allows viewers to look at the pictures from different camera angles.

▶ Digital TV allows the viewer to select a camera angle

■ Digital and conventional cameras

Digital cameras are used to record images in digital format. The images are stored on some kind of magnetic or optical media and can be downloaded directly onto a PC for editing or enhancing. The storage media is usually a smart card which can be used in a PC with an adapter or a memory stick.

Graphics programs such as Adobe Photoshop or Microsoft Photodraw can be used to manipulate digital images. The quality of a picture taken by a digital camera is limited by the amount of memory and the optical quality of the lens. Resolution refers to the sharpness of the image. The higher the resolution the more defined the picture will be. Pictures taken at high resolution take up more storage space than those taken

▲ A Kodak 512 MB memory card

at a lower resolution. Pictures taken at high resolution and printed on a low resolution printer will be limited to the resolution of the printer.

▶ Printing from a digital camera

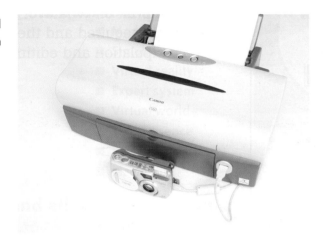

Most digital cameras come with an LCD screen which can be used to view the subject being photographed. Other features include the capability to record small digital movies in MPEG format and high powered optical zoom which allows objects at a distance to be photographed clearly.

Conventional cameras record pictures onto film. The film has to be developed and the photographs printed by a specialist. In general photographs produced from film are of a better quality than those produced on a digital camera.

The digital camera versus the conventional camera:

Digital Camera	Conventional Camera
Expensive to buy.	Cheaper to buy.
Photos taken can be downloaded to a PC and edited or manipulated using a graphics package.	Only hardcopy of photographs is produced.
Not all photos need to be printed. The user can delete unwanted photos from memory and print only the ones required.	All photos in the film have to be printed. This can be wasteful and expensive if the photos are not of good quality.
No expensive developing costs, the digital photos can be printed on a home computer printer.	The film from the camera has to be taken to a specialist so that photos can be printed. This is an expensive process.
No waiting to see photos. They can be viewed on the LCD screen immediately.	The photographer has to wait until photos are developed before viewing them.
The quality of photos can vary according to the output device producing them.	Photos produced are of a very high quality.
Photos are generally created in jpeg format and can be emailed or placed into other documents.	Hardcopy of the photos have to be scanned if they are to be used in digital documents.

these prices. Generally computers are very good at keeping track of information to assist managers and shop staff in decision–making. The following points summarise why shops use computers:

● to assist in stock control
● to order new stock
● to calculate profit margins
● to assist managers in decision-making.

■ The application of EFTPOS systems in shops

Try to imagine large shops without Electronic Funds Transfer Point of Sale (EFTPOS) terminals. This could mean that some activities will take a long time to carry out and even introduce the risk of human error into their information system. For example, if the price of an item changes it means having to change the price ticket on individual items. This in turn could lead to the same item with different prices, or even all items with the wrong price. If we investigate further you will find other drawbacks in shops such as the checkout operator keying in the wrong price of a product at the checkout, leading to human error and resulting in either undercharging or overcharging a customer.

For managers stock control would be difficult because it would mean having to record stock levels manually. There is no easy way of recording the stock levels as purchases are made. Some shops like to use loyalty cards to monitor customer spending habits in return for customer rewards. Without an EFTPOS keeping track of customer spending and shopping habits will be impossible.

Some customers like to pay for their goods using credit/debit cards and if the shop did not have magnetic stripe readers, purchases using credit cards and debit cards will be difficult, as the process could not automatically check customer details leading to increased security risks.

The disadvantages to a shop without a EFTPOS are:

● difficulty changing the price of a product
● increased risk of human error at the checkout
● difficulty in carrying out stock control activities
● impossibility of monitoring customer spending habits
● increased security risks of accepting customer credit/debit cards.

By using EFTPOS systems shops can overcome these problems and many more. When using EFTPOS systems shops can make use of barcode readers to record stock purchases, to check the price of a product, to allow customers to "self scan" as they shop and to allow staff to check stock using shelf edge labels. These shops can also use magnetic stripe readers or **chip and PIN** devices to automatically accept credit/debit card

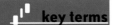
key terms

POS
An ordinary checkout till is referred to as a Point of Sale terminal.

EPOS
A checkout connected to a computer with a barcode reader is referred to as an Electronic Point of Sale terminal.

EFTPOS
A checkout connected to a computer with a barcode reader which can transfer money from a customers account using a credit/bank card is referred to as an Electronic Funds Transfer Point of Sale terminal.

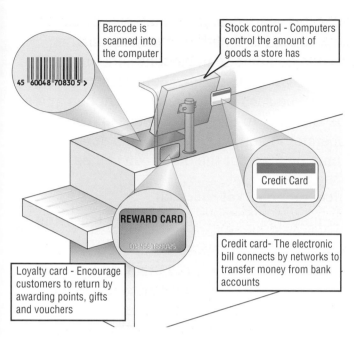

▲ Control at the shop checkout

purchases and to allow customers to make use of loyalty cards. Using the computer system also allows for immediate updating of stock records, ordering new stock and assisting managers in making decisions.

■ Components of a typical EFTPOS system

The components of a typical EFTPOS include:

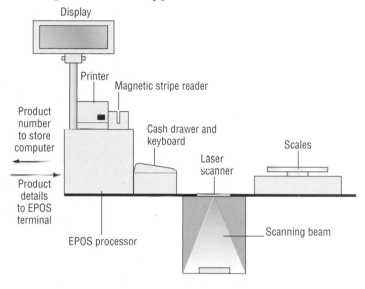

Barcode readers

When products are delivered to a shop the manufacturer includes a barcode as part of the package. Also shops that supply their own products, such as fresh provisions, will use their own in-house barcode system. Each product normally contains a unique barcode consisting of 13 digits. The information on a typical barcode usually contains product code, manufacturer code, country of origin and a check digit. The layout of a typical barcode is:

▲ Layout of a typical barcode

When barcodes are created digits are coded as a series of light and dark vertical bars of varying width. Although humans cannot determine a product from its barcode, the rate of accuracy from the barcode reader at the checkout is high. The barcode can be read by a handheld scanner

Barcodes use check digit validation (see page 147).

or a laser scanner (normally at checkouts in supermarkets). The barcode reader uses laser beam light to read and enter the code details automatically. When a barcode (remember all barcodes are unique!) is scanned it is matched with a record held on the shops computer system where other data can be retrieved such as a product description and a price, which will allow the customer to receive an itemised receipt and also assist the checkout operator in verifying the scanned details. If a barcode is damaged it cannot be read but the digits can still be keyed in.

Barcode scanning at a typical supermarket checkout

Each time a barcode is scanned at a EFTPOS terminal the following activities occur:

- The barcode scanner reads the barcode on the product.
- The barcode is sent to branch's computer (containing the stock database) by the EFTPOS terminal.
- The computer uses the barcode to search the stock file looking for a matching product.
- When the product is found, the product price and product description are sent back to the EFTPOS terminal.
- The branch's computer updates the stock level for the product to show that one (or more) has been sold.
- The good's price and description are displayed at the EFTPOS terminal and printed on a receipt.

▶ Use of barcode

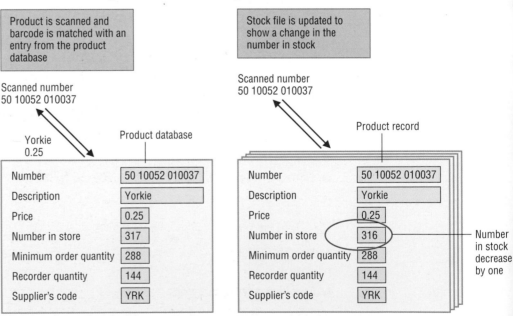

Apart from their use in shops, barcodes are also used to:

- track parcels in the post office
- track luggage in airports
- issue books in libraries.

Electronic Funds Transfer

This is a process of paying for goods without the need for having *real money* in your purse or wallet. It normally involves the customer using a credit card or a debit card, which contains a magnetic stripe and/or a chip. The EFTPOS terminal contains a magnetic stripe reader, which is used to carry out the transaction. Customer bank account details are entered from the stripe and the amount of the transaction is also entered, either automatically or it is keyed in. To verify the transaction the customer is normally asked to check and sign the transaction slip. Due to concerns with forging signatures many shops are moving towards a new system of *chip and PIN*. This involves them using the chip on the card to access customer details and then the customer will enter their PIN number to verify the transaction. Other EFT security concerns have meant some shops introducing an alternative to a customer signature, such as finger printing. Even though security is a concern to both the customer and the shop, there are many advantages of using EFT to both the customer and the shop.

Advantages of EFT to the customer

- Customers get their credit card slips automatically printed at the checkout.
- Customers using debit cards can also obtain cash at the checkout.
- The money involved in the transaction is debited from your account immediately so the balance displayed in your account is always up to date.
- Some customers feel more personal security if they don't have to carry large amounts of cash in their wallet/purse.
- Changing money into other currencies when abroad is not an issue.

Advantages of EFT to the vendor

- Payment into the shop's bank account is guaranteed as long as the transactions are properly authorised.
- Less administration/ paperwork with EFT so less staff required.
- Reduced concerns with forged monies.
- The shop collects less cash so there is less chance of theft.
- If the money is deposited immediately into the shops bank account they may receive more interest.

■ Automatic Teller Machines (ATM)

Sometimes these are referred to as the *hole in the wall* machines. Each bank operates and maintains their own network of ATMs. These networks are classified as wide area networks (WANs). ATMs are normally located outside each main branch of a bank. Nowadays they are also found in large shopping centres and even in large supermarkets. They allow a customer to gain access to their account 24 hours a day, 7 days a week. In other words they never close. ATMs allow an increasing range of activities to take place, such as:

■ Airlines

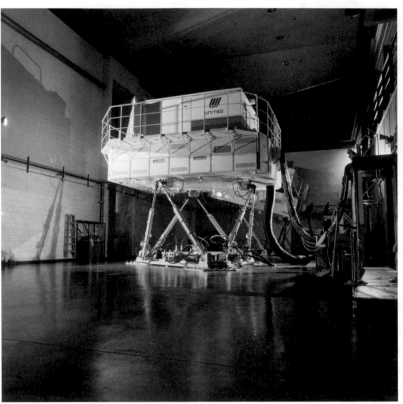

▲ A flight simulator

Training a pilot to fly an aeroplane can be both dangerous and expensive. If a pilot were trained entirely using a *real* aeroplane it would be expensive in terms of fuel costs and loss of possible airfares by taking a plane out of service. More importantly if the pilot makes a mistake the plane may crash resulting in loss of life. Therefore aircraft simulators can save money and are much safer to use in training. They also give the pilot an experience of a range of *real* environments.

Although the simulator does not look like an aeroplane in its physical appearance, it is a full size replica of a typical cockpit, but never leaves the ground. Computer screens replace the windows of the cockpit. The simulator is programmed to give the trainee pilot all the experiences he/she may or may not experience in the air. It is also used to provide continued training to experienced pilots. These experiences may include:

- turbulence, thunderstorms, snowstorms
- landing a plane on an icy runway
- flying a plane with only one engine working
- creating different types of faults on the plane to give the pilot the experience of dealing with emergencies
- flying a plane in thick fog
- landing at different airports around the world using high quality graphics showing the layout of runways and the surrounding environment.

It creates the illusion of *real* flying using *real* airports. The inputs to the system will be the control devices in the cockpit and a computer would monitor the settings of these. All the pilot's actions are recorded by the computer system and are used to provide feedback to the pilot.

■ Medicine

In the medical world, body scanners are available to collect large amounts of data about a person's internal system and biological make up. A computer can then process this data to produce a 3–D model of the whole or part of the body, creating a *virtual patient*.

This can be useful as it allows a surgeon to investigate a person's medical problem in detail before carrying out surgery. Surgeons can then plan and practise (simulate) a particular operation on the "virtual patient" in order to learn how to do this operation, before actually carrying it out on a real patient. This is sometimes known as *telepresence*. The surgeon can also consult with other specialists around the world by using computer technology such as video conferencing.

▶ An MRI scan

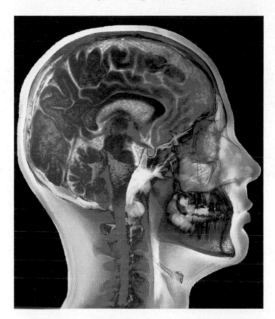

Another use of virtual reality in medicine is in the area of training medical students. An example of this would be to give the medical students an experience of what it is like to be exhausted from a medical illness such as undergoing chemotherapy to cure cancer. This would involve the medical student being placed on a specially designed chair with foot pedals and making use of an HMD. Using virtual reality they are placed in a typical house, where they can see the layout of the house through the headset.

The computer makes the student carry out relatively simple tasks through simulations, such as making the student answer the door when a bell rings. When they move, the student will realise that the pedals are designed to be difficult to move, giving the impression of how difficult it is for a patient to do this simple task. The image on the headset can also be continuously altered with different levels of vision from good vision to blurred vision giving the impression of dizziness.

This makes the new doctor aware of the problems patients will have when suffering a serious illness.

■ Gaming

Many computer games are designed with virtual reality.

For example when you play a football game on a computer you are simulating a real game such as a World Cup final. On the other hand you can have simulations without a computer, such as Monopoly for buying and selling *real* properties.

Computer games involve the designer programming a set of rules (model) for the user to follow. These rules could define a character in a game including features such as: the appearance of a character, how fast the character can run, how high the character can jump and how strong the character is. If weapons are involved more rules are included defining the range of weapons to be used, the range of fire of each weapon and the kinds of terrain the game is set on.

Sometimes these game simulations are realistic such as Formula One car racing games using *real* racing circuits. The game works by responding to inputs from the user devices including the throttle, the gears and the steering wheel. The user is given the impression of driving a real car including the visual, sound effects and the sensation of acceleration.

More games involving virtual reality are appearing in amusement arcades, such as using skis on a ski game to give the user a more realistic experience.

Computers in control

■ Sensors and data logging

A sensor is an input device, which can be used to measure almost any physical quantity. Different types of sensors are used to measure different physical quantities. Light sensors can measure light intensity, temperature sensors can measure temperature and sound sensors can measure the level of noise. In other words sensors measure changes in environmental conditions.

Data logging is the automatic capture and storage of data, without human intervention. A computer normally collects data at regular time intervals depending on the requirements of the application, without the need for human supervision. This can happen twenty-four hours a day, seven days a week, in a continuous way. The use of computers to log data is more accurate, and in some cases safer, than a human collecting data. Data can be stored over a period of time and then analysed by special or dedicated software. Sensors are used in data logging to obtain data automatically.

Since physical quanties such as temperature and light are continuously varying quanties they are described as analogue signals whereas computers can only process digital signals. Therefore there needs to be some form of analogue to digital conversion. The diagram below illustrates why light is an analogue signal. It shows a plot of light intensity detected by a light-sensitive device whose output is a voltage that varies with the intensity.

▶ Varying light intensity

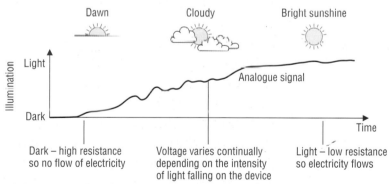

■ Analogue to digital conversion

An interface, or electrical device, called an Analogue to Digital Converter (ADC) is used to change analogue data into digital data. The analogue data is best described as a varying voltage whereas the digital signal is best described as a digital/binary pulse. To allow these computers to be used in data logging applications, the ADC is connected between the sensor and the computer.

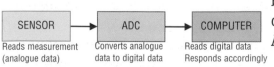

▲ Digitising real-world measurements

SIGNAL	DESCRIPTION
	Analogue signal.
	The physical quantity being measured can have many different values.
	It is a continuous signal.
	Digital signal/Pulse.
	Computers are not able to understand analogue data. They can only work with digital data (in binary format). Therefore the analogue data must be converted to digital format so it can be processed.

> Computer systems that can monitor their own activity by controlling their outputs according to their inputs, are said to have feedback.

To summarise, the following table illustrates the difference between an analogue and digital signal.

The principle of feedback

Feedback is an important concept in computer control. To illustrate feedback we will consider a home heating system, which uses a temperature sensor to measure room temperature at regular intervals, and the data fed into the computer. When the computer processes the data one of two possible outputs will occur, either to turn the heating on or turn the heating off.

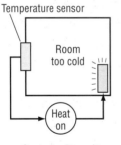
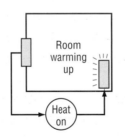
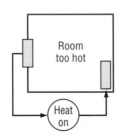

Temperature sensor

Room too cold — Heat on
Control unit monitors sensor reading and switches on heating

Room warming up — Heat on
As room warms, control unit continues to monitor the sensor output

Room too hot — Heat on
Sensor reading now shows that the room has reached the correct temperature, and the heating is turned off

▲ Basic feedback principle

To summarise the diagram we can say that if the temperature sensor says it is cold the heating is turned on. This will lead to a rise in temperature. When the temperature reaches a certain limit the sensor will tell the computer to turn the heat off.

We will now examine how computers are used in the following control applications:

- Greenhouse control systems
- Traffic control systems
- Domestic control systems

Greenhouse control systems

To guarantee success when growing plants they must be in a controlled environment. When computers are used in greenhouses sensors are required to measure temperature, light, humidity and dampness in soil. Therefore to allow the plants to grow well, each of the above measurements must be kept within pre-set limits. For example if we consider temperature, the computer must be programmed with an acceptable upper and lower value for greenhouse temperature, such that above the upper value it would be too hot and below the lower value it would be too cold. Therefore computer control is used to ensure measurements are always within these pre-set limits.

The sensors used are measuring physical quantities such as the amount of light in the greenhouse at any one time. A typical light sensor (which is technically known as a *light-dependent resistor*) measuring light throughout day and night may produce the following data:

▶ Light intensity variations

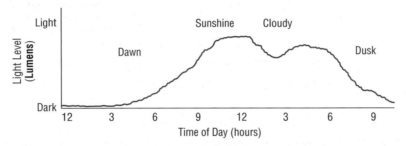

When the amount of natural light falls the computer may turn on the lights in the greenhouse and again when the amount of natural light increases the computer may turn off the lights in the greenhouse. If there is too much natural light the computer may also control the amount of light by opening and closing blinds.

As the temperature sensor measures temperature the computer controlled activities may result in turning fans on and off, or even opening and closing windows automatically, if the greenhouse gets too hot. If the temperature goes below the lower limits the computer could turn on heaters and again turn the heaters off when the temperature rises to an acceptable level.

With regards to humidity the sensor will measure how much water vapour is in the air and the computer controlled activity could be to turn on or off the water sprinklers. The same process could apply to the soil sensors.

To summarise, if the value sensed is outside the range known to the computer, then a signal will be sent to activate a device (normally an actuator), which will bring the value back within the range. Therefore the computer-controlled greenhouse uses the principle of feedback.

■ Computers systems in traffic control

These computer controlled systems are mainly employed in large cities where traffic is a problem. The main aim of these systems is to keep traffic moving, particularly during rush hours in the early morning or evening. Computers are used in different aspects of traffic control such as traffic lights, car park management and vehicle speeding.

In cities traffic lights are normally controlled at a central location. Each set of traffic lights can be programmed to vary in operation throughout a day. For example a lot of traffic may arrive into the city in the morning, therefore the lights can be programmed to remain green on roads into a city for longer periods in the morning. Again in the evening, traffic lights out of the city can remain green for longer. The sequence during the rest of the day can also vary if the need arises. These systems are often called **vehicle actuation systems**.

Sensors can be placed on roads to detect and count the cars over a period of time. This data is then sent back to the main computer, which in turn can send signals back to the lights that amend the timings of the light sequence. In the case of emergency vehicles such as fire engines, it would even be possible to ensure that the traffic lights are all green along its path.

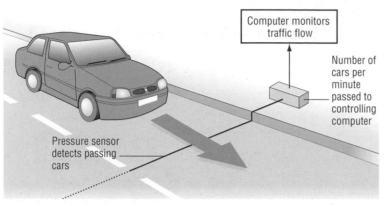

Computer monitors traffic flow

Number of cars per minute passed to controlling computer

Pressure sensor detects passing cars

▲ Pneumatic pressure sensor detects passing vehicles

Although most control of traffic lights in cities is centralised, each set of lights can also react automatically to local events such as people wishing to cross roads. By pressing a button, the local control box will allow the lights to be changed to red for a short period of time.

To assist in maintenance, traffic lights can be monitored, allowing faults to be detected automatically leading to prompt repairs.

In the area of car park management computer controlled systems can direct cars around a city to those car parks with available space. The system can calculate the number of vehicles entering

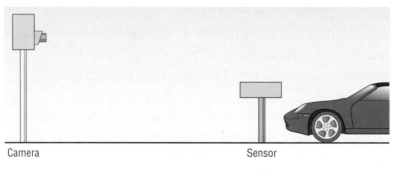

Camera   Sensor

▲ A speed camera

and leaving a car park at regular time intervals, and then display on large electronic signposts the number of empty spaces in a named car park. Sensors are used to log each car on entry and exit automatically.

As speed becomes a major issue on our roads, police forces are making more use of computer technology to sense and record the speeds of individual cars.

This computer–controlled system consists of sensors, which are capable of detecting car speeds and if the speed is excessive a camera automatically takes a photograph of the car including registration number, speed, location and the time and date of incident. All these details can be superimposed on the photograph. Using the registration plate the owner can easily be found and a copy of the photo sent, with a fine and police follow up.

The data logged by each camera can also be analysed to produce data about those roads where speeding is a problem. Special sensors built into traffic lights can also detect cars driving through red traffic lights.

■ Domestic control systems

When a computer is used to control a device in your home, by using a microprocessor, which is inside the device, it is described as an **embedded computer**. These devices include washing machines, burglar alarms, video recorders, and microwave ovens, only to mention some of the modern house appliances.

The embedded computer in each device will control the input and output devices attached to the device. Consider a typical automatic washing machine. When the user selects a washing program the microprocessor carries out a pre-stored sequence of instructions. The microprocessor will carry out activities such as turning on and off switches for water intake and outlet, controlling the water heater to heat the water to a certain temperature, controlling the water pump and controlling the drum. To do all of these activities a number of sensors are used including water flow sensors, temperature sensors and door open/close sensors. During the washing cycle computer controlled motors and pumps will also be used. The diagram below indicates the inputs, processes and outputs in a typical washing machine.

▶ Components of a typical washing machine

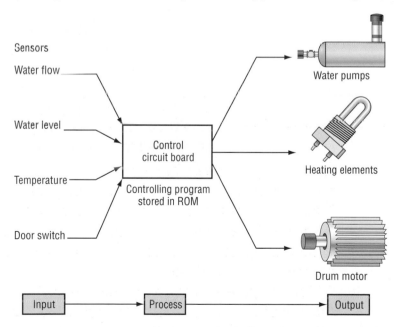

On-line services applications

E-commerce is defined as ... *conducting business transactions over electronic networks* ....

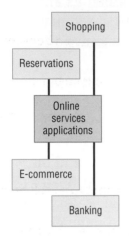

▲ Online services

The arrival of communications technology has changed the way a business operates and the ways in which customers do their business. A simple example is when a business advertises. They include their web address and their email address and when a customer shops they may order using the Internet.

Online services include situations where a customer or a business performs transactions electronically. For example, people now book flights using the Internet which involves a customer enquiring about a flight, getting a cost for a flight, booking the flight, paying for the flight using EFT methods and printing an e-ticket as evidence of booking.

When shopping online customers can visit *virtual shops* to view goods, place them into electronic shopping baskets and pay using EFT methods and normally receive the goods within 48 hours. To increase security businesses are now encrypting customer financial details. Internet shopping will never fully replace traditional shopping as there is no provision for social interaction or handling the goods before their bought by customers. Many shops offer loyalty cards which are used to encourage shoppers by giving cash back and discount off goods. In return shops can track customer shopping habits and control their stock to meet customer demands.

When customers order goods and services online this is done using a technique referred to as electronic data interchange (EDI) which is a system aimed at sending orders, paying invoices and sending information electronically.

The major high street banks encourage their customers to bank online through the Internet or telephone banking. Customers can maintain their own accounts without having to pay bank fees such as setting up standing orders and transferring money from one account to another account. The customers are even paid by their employers using EFT.

Advantages and disadvantages of using online services for a business

There are many advantages and disadvantages of using online services within a business environment.

Advantages

- Worldwide client access, meaning a business can attract a larger customer base, both locally and globally.
- A business has the ability to communicate with customers immediately such as supplying product information and specifications through online electronic catalogues which include graphics.

- The use of the Internet allows a business to advertise new products and current promotions cheaply compared to using national newspapers.
- New clients can be found without the need for employing salespeople.
- Update product information frequently and immediately.
- Quick and cheap method of doing market research on customer views.
- Assess the impact of Internet by using a count of those who visit the site.

Disadvantages

- Due to business people working from home, lack of human interaction between employees can lead to feelings of isolation.
- Modern technology can be expensive to purchase and maintain for a business.

■ Advantages and disadvantages of using online services for a customer

Advantages

- Internet is now readily available on a home PC including cheaper local call access anywhere in the world.
- Growing volumes of Information on a wide variety of topics such as electronic catalogues.
- Valuable learning resource for customers because Internet skills may be required for their jobs.
- A range of product reviews can be obtained before you decide to make a purchase.
- Goods are normally cheaper than buying on the high street. Customers normally get free delivery when they purchase a certain amount.
- You can buy goods from anywhere in the world which means you are not restricted to shopping in your own town or city.
- Search engines can assist the user to precisely locate what they need.
- Multimedia format of the Internet makes it attractive and easier for customers to use.
- Other services such as email can be used by customers to request more information.

Disadvantages

- No guarantee the information on a website is accurate or up to date.
- Large amount of undesirable material such as pornography is readily available.
- Large telephone bills can result if Internet is used during peak hours.
- Excessive time on Internet could result in a lack of interaction with others, leading to a decline in social skills.
- Going online runs the risk of hackers gaining access to your personal details or downloading a virus onto your hard drive.
- Using only a keyword or inappropriate searching techniques in a search engine may make it difficult to find appropriate information.
- Many customers are worried about credit card fraud when buying goods.

Questions C2 (a–d)
Questions on ICT Components

1 Copy and complete the table below:

Acronym	Expand
RAM	
ROM	
ATM	
CD-ROM	
PDA	
VDU	
ASCII	
EPOS	
WORM	
GUI	

2 Name **three** components of a CPU.

3 a) Explain the difference between ROM and RAM.
   b) For each, suggest a suitable use.

4 Briefly outline the purpose of the *bootstrapping* program.

5 Name **two** different types of *keying in* devices, and for each suggest a suitable use.

6 Describe **two** different devices that could be used as an alternative to a mouse.

7 State **three** advantages of using a digital camera over a traditional camera for input.

8 State **two** advantages of using a touch screen over a keyboard for an inexperienced user.

9 Distinguish between *hard copy* output and *soft copy* output.

10 State **two** disadvantages of using LCD screens over ordinary desktop monitors.

11 Distinguish between the terms *pixel* and *resolution* when describing a VDU.

12 State four criteria that can be used when you are purchasing a printer.

13 For a floppy disk:
   a) Suggest a suitable storage capacity.
   b) State **two** reasons why IT users need a floppy disk drive.
   c) State **two** disadvantages of a floppy disk compared to a CD-ROM.

14 Suggest **two** uses for a hard disk on a typical PC.

15 a) State **three** different types of optical disks.
   b) Briefly describe how data is written to a CD-ROM.

Questions for Section C2b Information Systems

All questions in this section are for use with Full course candidates.

1 Complete the table below, expanding the acronyms or abbreviation:

Acronym or abbreviation	Expanded	Meaning
ASCII		
csv	Comma separated variable	
dpi		
gif		
jpeg		
mpeg		
OMR		
OCR		
rtf		
Tiff (higher tier only)		
Pict (higher tier only)		

2 Make a leaflet which outlines the key features of good form design.

Higher tier extension
Include in your leaflet an example of a well-designed form and a poorly designed form. You could find these forms on the Internet or bring examples of forms from home.

3 Use the spell checker and word count facilities in your word processor to check the leaflet you have produced in question 2 above.

Higher Tier Extension
Record the results of each by using screen shots of the output and comment on your accuracy level.

4 Data checking is a very important aspect of ensuring that data is correct. Create a multimedia presentation which will outline the different types of validation which can be used when entering data into a system

Higher Tier Extension
Your presentation should distinguish between validation and verification.

5 A skateboard company keeps records of its products and the suppliers who supply the products and are thinking about putting the data into a relational database.
a) What is a relational database?
b) Why would you not advise the company to keep the data in a flat file system.

Higher Tier Extension
Your answer to b) above should include the terms *data redundancy* and *data integrity*.
c) What are the purpose of relationships in a relational database.

6 The company above decides to design a database with the following two tables:

Supplier table   Product table

  a) Suggest six fields for each table and give the data type you would select for each field.

  b) Design an on-screen form which will capture the details for a new product.

Higher Tier Extension

  c) Suggest a key field for each table.

  d) Suggest validation which should be carried out for each field.

7 Data can be input directly to a computer using data capture.

  a) Describe TWO data capture techniques you have studied.

  b) For each make a list of the advantages and disadvantages.

Higher Tier Extension

  c) For each method give two examples of where it is used, describing how human error is minimised.

8 a) Describe how a check digit works in data verfication.

Higher Tier Extension Task

  b) Calculate the check digit for this book. (You will not be asked to calculate a check digit in your examination).

9 a) What is the difference between *information* and *data*?

  b) Give two examples of information and data.

10 a) What is data compression?

Higher Tier Extension

  b) Why is data compression carried out?

  c) Give three examples of where data compression is done.

  d) What does the term *data portability* mean?

  e) In relation to graphics, describe what is meant by *resolution*.

Higher Tier Extension Task

  f) Find three examples of graphics created at different resolutions and comment on the differences between each picture.

11 a) Using a graphics package create a logo for the company in question 5. Save the logo as *myskatelogo.bmp* – a bitmap.

  b) Using the same graphics package open *myskatelogo.bmp* and convert it to a jpeg. Save it as *myskatelogo.jpg*.

  c) Examine the properties of *myskatelogo.bmp* and *myskatelogo.jpg*. Take screen shots of the properties and comment on the difference in size and quality.

Higher Tier Extension

  d) Make a list of all the differences you have found between *myskatelogo.bmp* and *myskatelogo.jpg*.

  e) Describe why a jpeg might be more suitable for use on a web page.

Questions for C2(c) Digital Communication Systems

Acronym	Expand
LAN	
WAN	
WWW	
ISP	
HTML	
URL	
ISDN	
PSTN	
ADSL	
PC	

1 a) What is a LAN?
   b) Draw a diagram of how a LAN might be organised.
   c) What topology have you used in your LAN?
   d) Briefly describe the way in which this type of LAN works.
   e) What are the advantages and disadvantages associated with it?

Higher Tier Extension   f) What are the roles of switches and hubs in a LAN?

2 Full course only question
   a) In order for networks to communicate there are communication *protocols*. Explain this term.
   b) Explain why communication protocols are required.
   c) Networks must keep data secure. How can this be achieved?
   d) What is the function of a router on a network?

3 a) What is a WAN?
   b) What are the main differences between a LAN and a WAN?

Higher Tier Extension   c) What are the advantages of a company having a WAN?

4 Full Course question only.

As an Internet user you have been asked to provide a new Internet user with information on the equipment and software required for Internet connection.

Prepare a multimedia presentation which will show the new user what equipment and software is required for Internet connection. Make sure you give the purpose of each piece of equipment. (You could use pictures from the Internet to make your presentation more appealing.)

Higher Tier Extension   Add to your presentation three slides which will comment on the speed, costs and bandwidth of three different Internet connection types.

5 a) What is the difference between the World Wide Web and the Internet?

   b) What is an *intranet*?

   c) How can students and teachers at your school or college benefit from using an intranet?

   d) Describe how video conferencing could be used in education.

Higher Tier Extension

What are the similarities and differences between an intranet site and an Internet site?

6 Compare email and fax under the following headings:
   - Cost
   - Technologies required
   - Facilities offered

Higher Tier Extension

Give three situations where email would not be suitable to use as a communications tool.

7 Full course question only.

Mobile phones provide a variety of communications facilities.

   a) Make a list of these and describe how they could be used by a student travelling to and from university weekly.

Higher Tier Extension

   b) Portable hand-held devices are used by businessmen to contact the office when they are away. Describe three facilities which they can use for business purposes.

8 Digital imaging systems have become more popular in recent years as technology has become cheaper.

   a) Compare digital TV with analogue TV.

   b) What are the advantages of using a digital camera instead of a conventional camera?

Higher Tier Extension

Explain how data is transferred between digital cameras and computers and describe the advantages of using this facility.

Questions on Applications of ICT

All questions are from Higher Tier CCEA papers.

1 Copy and complete the table below:

Acronym	Expand
EPOS	
DAC	
EDI	
PIN	
EFTPOS	
MICR	
HMD	
MODEM	
ADC	
LDR	

2 Suggest **three** reasons why a supermarket uses a bar coding system.

3 List **five** different hardware devices that are included in a typical EFTPOS.

4 State **four** different contents of a barcode on a supermarket product.

5 Apart from supermarkets, state **two** other applications that use barcodes.

6 State **three** activities available to a customer at an ATM.

7 State **two** differences between a magnetic stripe card and a smart card.

8 What is meant by the term *chip and PIN*.

9 Describe what happens during *batch processing* in a typical application.

10 Describe how computer simulations are used in **two** different ICT applications.

11 Explain the purpose of an Analogue to Digital Converter (ADC) when using a computer to sense temperature in a greenhouse.

12 Using an ICT application, explain the principle of feedback.

13 Describe **two** different uses of computer systems in traffic control.

14 Discuss the implications to the consumer of using computers for:
a) shopping online
b) banking online

15 Explain the impact of e-commerce to a retail outlet on the high street.

13 Implications of ICT for individuals, organisations and society

C3a

▶ In this section you will learn about the effects that ICT systems have on your lives. You will look at how ICT has made education, employment and home and leisure activities different.

▶ The increase in the use of ICT for keeping personal information has led to the development of laws designed to protect the public. You will learn about the main features of these laws and the effect they have had on the workplace in the areas of data protection and health and safety.

▶ You need to learn the definitions of these terms:

- Anti-glare screen/filter
- Computer Misuse Act
- Copyright Designs and Patents Act
- Data logging
- Data Protection Act
- Digital recording equipment
- Digital television

- E-commerce
- Ergonomically
- MP3 file
- Hacking
- Software piracy
- Telecommuting
- Teleworking
- Downloading software

- Software licence
- Internet cookie
- Personal data
- Video conferencing
- Virus

▶ You need to expand all of these acronyms:

- CD-ROM
- CD
- LAN
- WAN
- DVD

- MIDI
- RSI
- ELF
- MPEG
- MP3

- POS
- EFT
- FAST

The impact of ICT on education

The twenty-first century classroom makes use of many aspects of technology to help with teaching and learning. A single computer in the classroom can provide pupils with a wide variety of experiences and gives the teacher a sophisticated teaching tool.

Pupils can use these tools to create high quality and well-presented homeworks, projects and coursework. Teachers can use them to develop better quality teaching materials.

A screen from the CAL package *Everyone's a winner* which teaches students about the technicalities of soccer in preparation for a graded examination in PE.

Interactive subject-specific learning materials are produced on CD-ROM. Multimedia software presents onscreen moving pictures and sounds. Pupils can watch and learn within a stimulating environment. Special subject-specific packages like *Geometry Inventor* for mathematics and encyclopedias like *Encarta* on CD-ROM provide an additional information source in the classroom.

Pupils can use these individually while the teacher is working with the rest of the class. Some Computer Assisted Learning (CAL) packages can teach a topic in a multimedia environment. They can then assess students and allow them to learn at their own pace. These packages can automatically record student performance for the teacher to monitor.

Science and technology make use of data logging equipment which uses sensors over a period of time to collect data. Data recorded using this equipment is accurate and can be processed by a computer to produce information or to draw graphs. CD writers and MIDI assist in learning and producing music and DVD technology provides students with interactive films and real-life learning situations.

A data projector can project the computer screen on to a large whiteboard. It makes the single computer into a whole class teaching tool. This lets all of the pupils see a particular demonstration at once.

Using a data projector and an interactive whiteboard, pupils can interact with the computer by pressing or clicking on the board. This allows students to collaborate on projects in a single group.

A data projector

▲ Using a) data projection, and b) whiteboard in the classroom

Technology can assist students with special educational needs or learning difficulties. There are accessibility tools built into many school networks. Examples of these are:

- magnifier – magnifies text so that sight-impaired students can read it
- on screen keyboard – gives students with low mobility a keyboard onscreen; Letters can be typed by simply rolling the mouse over the letter
- voice recognition software – can be trained to understand the spoken word; These sounds are spoken into a microphone and the computer can be operated by speaking instead of using the mouse or keyboard
- braille keyboards and printers – can be incorporated to assist blind students in the use of technology
- talking word processors – can help students with learning difficulties to produce error free documents
- concept keyboards and trackerball mouse devices – can help those with limited mobility to manipulate the hardware and software
- highly sophisticated movement sensors – can sense eye or muscle movement and allow people with little or no mobility to make use of a computer.

▶ The onscreen keyboard which can be used with Windows applications

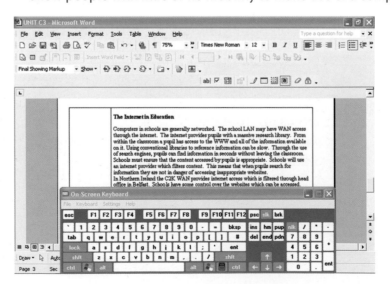

The Internet in Education

Computers in schools are generally networked. The school LAN may have WAN access through the Internet. The Internet provides pupils with a massive research library. From within the classroom a pupil has access to the WWW and all of the information available on it. Using conventional libraries to reference information can be slow. Through the use of search engines, pupils can find information in seconds without leaving the classroom. Schools must ensure that the content accessed by pupils is appropriate. Schools will use an Internet provider which filters content. This means that when pupils search for information they are not in danger of accessing inappropriate websites.

In Northern Ireland the schools' C2K WAN provides Internet access which is filtered through the head office in Belfast. Schools have some control over the websites which can be accessed. For example students and staff can be prevented from accessing Internet shopping or web email such as Yahoo! mail or Hotmail.

Communication technologies in education

The use of communications technologies provides new opportunities for distance learning. Students and teachers can use email as a means of communicating. Video conferencing allows students to take part in two-way visual communication. The possibilities for this type of technology is endless.

Schools could video conference with companies or other schools which are at opposite sides on the world. On a smaller scale, schools which are remotely situated could video conference with larger schools who might share their teachers and resources. Pupils can exchange ideas interactively and produce joint projects regardless of where their schools are located. Bulletin boards and controlled interactive text based discussion (similar to chat rooms) are also successfully used to allow the school community to extend beyond the school itself.

E-portfolios are a new technology which will allow pupils to create and maintain an electronic collection of projects and personal data. This would free them from gathering paper based evidence of completing coursework and personal achievements. An e-portfolio can be web based. A pupil can access it from school and home. A teacher can access it and assess the pupil's work online. Parents can become more informed about their child's progress by browsing the e-portfolio.

A Virtual Learning Environment (VLE) is a tool which is used in many universities to deliver courses using some of the technologies outlined.

The VLE also allows lecturers to assess students' work and even track their *attendance* record within the course itself.

One word which could encompass the use of all of these technologies in education is the term *e-learning* (electronic learning). This is the use of these technologies to enhance the learning experience of every student. The use of communications technology in education means that students have access to resources and teachers on a more flexible basis. The boundaries between home and school or university are blurred. Collaboration and collegiality between students and teachers from different establishments becomes possible.

The impact of ICT on employment

Information communication technologies have been introduced in many aspects of working life. This has meant changes in the way we do our jobs. In manufacturing, for example, the introduction of robots means that the work of a number of workers is being done by one machine. In general jobs which are highly repetitive and require a low level of skill can now be carried out by a robot or computer. Examples of this can be seen in:

- car manufacture – where paint spraying in car factories has been replaced by computer controlled robots
- warehouse work – where stock is moved from one place to another using computer-controlled fork-lift trucks
- in offices – where office workers make use of applications software packages to produce documents and communications technologies to deliver internal and external communications.

Reduced number of manual jobs

Increased unemployment

The opportunity of working from home

De-skilling or even elimination of some office jobs

The effect on the individual

The creation of new and interesting jobs

The opportunity to work for yourself

The need to continually update skills

▲ ICT and the individual

Changes in work patterns

The change in technology used has led to changing work patterns for employees and employers alike. Portable technology like laptops allows more people to take work home. Employees can be contacted at anytime using mobile telephones or PDAs. The working day is therefore extended and the boundaries between home and work become less defined. Many think that there is little distinction between home and work because of this.

Businesses who want to operate in the global marketplace must be available 24 hours a day because of the time difference between countries. This and the upsurge in 24-hour call centres and helplines means that staff have to work shifts during unsociable hours.

Some organisations make all internal communications by email. This means that a proportion of the employee's day must be set aside to read and answer emails.

Job displacement and retraining

Many manual jobs have been taken on by sophisticated ICT systems. For example:

- filing clerks have been replaced by databases coupled with networks to allow many terminals to access a common pool of data
- a skilled typist who made few mistakes as the data was entered onto pages (one mistake would result in retyping the whole document) has been replaced by word processing.

With few skills in word processing we can produce a professional document.

In a changing work environment many people require retraining to enable them to do their job with technology incorporated. In an office for example, workers have to be trained in the use of fax machines, a digital telephone switch board, photocopying and the use of software. They have to learn the new skills necessary to operate the new equipment. In offices nowadays the equipment changes from one year to the next and the skills required to operate it also change. People need to be re-trained to take account of changing technology.

In all areas of working life there is a continual need to update skills. The nature and the type of job people are doing is always changing. This has led to lifelong learning programmes. Employees must attend training courses on a regular basis throughout their working lives.

Job creation

New technologies have created new jobs. In order to design and maintain the technology we need programmers, software engineers, database administrators and network managers. The World Wide Web and the existence of websites has led to a new job title called web designer. Many of the manual jobs which have been lost are being replaced with jobs which require skills and knowledge to operate technology. Government surveys suggest that the use of ICT has created more jobs than have been lost through its use.

■ Home based employment

The use of communications technology has made working from home much easier. Employees can stay in touch with the office through the use of the Internet, email, video conferencing and WAP enabled hand-held devices like PDAs. Employees can also log on to a company's intranet from home. Working from home like this is called *teleworking*. People who work from home like this are called *teleworkers* or *telecommuters*.

As cities become more congested, people are demanding an alternative way of working. This has been made possible with advances in communications technology and networks such as fibre optics, faster modems, faxes, mail and teleconferencing.

What are the advantages of teleworking?

Advantage	
Cost	Saves on travel cost and travel time to and from work. The company is not liable for travel expenses.
Location	The employee can live anywhere. There is no necessity to live within travelling distance of work. The company can employ people with the right skills regardless of where they live.
Flexibility	The employee has flexible working hours and can carry out other activities such as child care.
Overheads	Organisations do not need to rent expensive city centre offices.
Society	The environment will benefit because there are fewer cars on the road which will help reduce pollution and traffic congestion. Prosperity is spread across a given country rather than concentrated in commuter belts near large cities.
Equality for disadvantaged people	Working from home will allow people with disabilities to carry out their jobs in an environment designed for them.

What are the disadvantages of teleworking?

Disadvantage	
Social interaction	Employees may feel isolated because of loss of social interaction. Employees may not have a good understanding of the company's aims and vision.
Discipline	Employees need an office or workroom at home. This may be difficult to find in a family home. Employees need to be disciplined to ensure that they distinguish between home and work activities. They need to work the required amount of time and complete tasks to deadline. This could be made difficult by interruptions at home.
Monitoring	Managers will find it more difficult to monitor employee activity and productivity.

Health and safety issues

Computers are fully integrated into the workplace. Millions of people work using computers for long periods every day. Like all machinery and equipment in the workplace, computers have to be used correctly and safely. The Health and Safety Regulations of 1992 define the law regarding health and safety standards for the use of computers at work. The law covers those using computers as part of their job, but not students at schools, universities or colleges.

There are a number of health problems and injuries which can arise because of the use of computers. It is the responsibility of an employer to provide a working environment which minimises the possibility of employees developing these problems. There are standards expected in areas such as:

- lighting
- furniture
- noise
- hardware
- software
- temperature control.

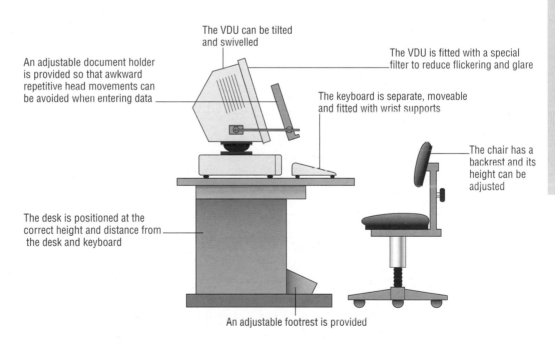

The VDU can be tilted and swivelled

The VDU is fitted with a special filter to reduce flickering and glare

An adjustable document holder is provided so that awkward repetitive head movements can be avoided when entering data

The keyboard is separate, moveable and fitted with wrist supports

The chair has a backrest and its height can be adjusted

The desk is positioned at the correct height and distance from the desk and keyboard

An adjustable footrest is provided

▲ Health and safety in the office

The following table describes these conditions and indicates how the organisation of furniture, lighting and choice of equipment can help to cut down on their effects.

Health problem	Description	How can it be reduced?
RSI	Repetitive Strain Injury Refers to a range of conditions affecting the neck, shoulders, arms and hands. The employee is forced to use the same muscle groups to perform the same actions over and over again such as working at a keyboard all day. This can result in a condition at the wrists known as *Carpel's Tunnel*.	● Taking regular breaks. ● Using ergonomically designed keyboard and mouse. ● Using appropriate furniture such as adjustable swivel chair. ● Using a wrist rest underneath the keyboard to avoid 'Carpel's Tunnel'. ● Use a foot rest. ● Change the sitting position from time to time.
Eyestrain	A very common problem caused by over exposure to computer screens. It can also lead to headaches, blurred vision and a deterioration in eyesight. This condition can cause discomfort leading to less work being done.	● Using anti-glare screen. ● Using swivel base on screen to deflect light. ● Using screen which has adjustable brightness and contrast. ● Having good lighting in the office. ● Using blinds to control sunlight. ● Employer providing regular free eye tests.
Back pain	Usually minor problems which can be debilitating periodically. The person may suffer back pain or immobility. The problem can be related to the sitting position at the computer.	● Using adjustable chair which allow height adjustment and backrest tilting. ● Take regular breaks and walk around to exercise muscles.
Radiation	Computer VDUs can give out Extremely Low Frequency (ELF) radiation. The strength is similar to mild sunlight exposure. Illness may occur if the user is working for long periods in front of a computer screen. There is some concern about pregnant women and the unborn child being exposed to computer radiation.	● Taking regular breaks. ● Using swivel screen to deflect the glare. ● Anti-glare filters. ● Using low-emission screen.

■ Safety in the workplace

The workplace must also be safe. A safe workplace means that employees will not meet with accidents because of the way in which the equipment is organised. Here are some measures employers can take to ensure the safety of their employees:

● Electricity switches, plugs, sockets and computer equipment should be in a good state of repair and regularly checked.
● Computer cables and network leads should be safely organised using cable management. This will prevent accidents such as tripping over cables and electrocution.
● Extension leads should not be used in the office as overloading of electrical sockets could result in a fire.
● The temperature in the room should be controllable. High temperatures could make computers overheat or employees uncomfortable causing stress or illness.
● Antistatic carpet should be used in the room to avoid the build up of electrostatic charge.
● Fire extinguishers which can put out electrical fires should be installed.
● Employees should not eat or drink near computers.
● Employees should be fully trained in the causes of accidents in the office and be made aware of the company policy on Health and Safety.

The impact of ICT on home and leisure

■ Digital TV

Digital TV offers viewers high quality sound and pictures in digital format. This type of transmission also includes many features not available in analogue television.

Feature	Explanation
More channels available	● Because of the bandwidth used by digital television more channels can be transmitted and viewed.
EPG	● Electronic programme guide, which allows viewers to see what programmes are being transmitted. The EPG usually gives some additional information about the programme.
Reduced interference	● Digital TV signals are not as prone to distortion through interference. This makes the pictures more clear and pleasant to view.
Pay per view	● Viewers can select programmes they wish to watch and pay for them if they are not part of the subscription package. Charges are usually made for key sporting events or new movies.
Digital recorders	● Viewers can record one channel while watching another using the TV top digibox.
Interactive TV	● Interactive TV allows the user to make purchases or interact online. Information can flow in both directions, from the user to the TV or from the TV to the user. Some facilities available on interactive TV include, games, home shopping and email.

Digital TV is no longer just a viewing service it is a fully integrated home communication service. Advances in technology, like the development of broadband have moved digital TV in this direction. Viewers expectations are higher in terms of quality of sound and picture and interactivity.

■ ICT in the music industry

What is MP3 and how does it work?

▶ An MP3 player
128 MB Capacity.
Voice recording function.
External FM Radio:
87.5–108 MHz.
96×26 pixel display.

Digital recordings of music are distributed on CD. Music files produced in this format are generally very large. The Internet is vastly becoming a major medium for the download of music both commercially and illegally. If music is to be downloaded in the same format as on CD it would take a long time and very fast Internet connections would be required. MP3 is another audio file format for storing music files. It is a compressed format which makes the size of a music file up to 12 times smaller that a conventional music file on CD. This is achieved by eliminating frequencies and sounds on the soundtrack which the human ear cannot normally hear. Music files in MP3 format can be downloaded from the Internet much quicker than music files in wav or aiff format.

▶ An MP4 Player
2.2 GB capacity.
2.5" (6.4 cm diagonal) TFT LCD Screen.
17 Hr Record time
ASV, jpeg, MP3, WAV format supported.

The development of MP3 technology means that more people are using the web to download music. Manufacturers have flooded the market with MP3 players which are tiny in size and can hold up to 100 songs. Users can download their favourite songs and store them on this tiny device. The songs can be overwritten again and again.

MP4 compression standards are now being developed by the MPEG (Moving Pictures Expert Group). This is the compression standard relating not only to sound but to moving images and multimedia as well. MP4 players can play sound and pictures or movies.

What is digital recording?

▶ The components of a digital recording/playback system

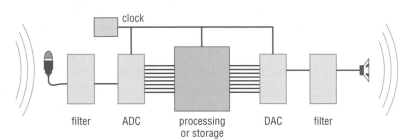

filter · ADC · processing or storage · DAC · filter

Since the invention of CDs music has been recorded and stored digitally. Digital recording involves taking the analogue sounds produced when playing music and converting them into digital signals. This is done using an Analogue to Digital Converter (ADC). It is the digital signals that are recorded onto the CD. When the music is played back, a Digital to Analogue Converter (DAC) changes the digital signals to analogue and these signals are amplified and sent to speakers.

The two main aims of digital recording are:

● To produce a recording which is highly similar to the original sound as it was played.
● To ensure that the music sounds the same each time it is played.

Digital music can be recorded from many sources, it does not always have to be a microphone. MIDI keyboards can be plugged into a PC and music can be recorded directly from them. This music can be mixed with digital music from any source therefore making it a very versatile way of producing music. Music which has been digitally encoded onto a CD is highly durable and minor damages to the CD will have no impact on the sound produced.

Digital recording can be carried out successfully on a PC given the correct peripherals and software.

Midi and sound effects

Musical Instrument Digital Interface or MIDI is a technology which allows musical instruments to be connected together or to a computer. Most MIDI keyboards can create sound from several instruments, for example flute, drums, violin and trumpet to name but a few. The notes or melodies composed are recorded as digital signals. These can be saved onto a computer or any digital storage medium. When they are loaded back onto the MIDI device it will play back the music which has been saved.

Digital music can be created by using the computer keyboard and mouse. Tracks made using different MIDI devices and the computer can be mixed together using computer software. This makes the creation of digital music using several different instruments easy for one person. The musician can record several different tracks using different instruments on the MIDI keyboard. These tracks can then be mixed to form a single track with several instruments being played at one time.

MIDI devices allow users to distort sound to produce sound effects. Notes played can be echoed, reverberated, lengthened or shortened. Most electronic instruments have their own sound effects built in. On a MIDI keyboard there are many sound effects like bells, beeps, chimes, whistles, and synthesizer functions which allow users to create their own sounds.

Because of the versatile nature of digital music, sound effects can be added to the music at a later stage to change the mood of the piece.

The advantages of using MIDI to produce music are:

- The sheet music will be generated automatically.
- The tempo, key and duration of the music can be changed easily.
- The instrument playing a particular section can be changed easily.
- Sound effects can be added after the music has been composed.
- Voice tracks can be integrated with the music.
- The music can be edited easily without having to rewrite the whole piece again.
- Once produced the music can be played on a device which has digital audio facilities.
- Music can be produced by people who are not experts.

The use of digital technology has revolutionised the music industry. Production techniques have changed, the way in which music is sold has changed and the technology used to listen to music has become personalised and portable ensuring every person can listen to their own selection of music from wherever they wish.

■ ICT in the games industry

The global games industry generates an income of $20 billion per year and is now widely recognised as a major part of the entertainment industry. Millions of games are sold every year at a cost of £30 to £50.

Computers are widely used in our homes to play games. Computer game playing is a higly popular leisure activity for young people. Games can be installed locally to the computer's hard disk and played using a wide variety of peripherals such as a joystick, a driving console, a game pad or a dance mat. Some games can be played online between players all over the world.

As well as using a computer, games can also be played on specialised gaming consoles. Examples of these consoles are:

- Dreamcast
- Sony playstation (PS1 and PS2)
- Microsoft X-box
- Nintendo Gamecube
- portable gaming, such as a Gameboy Advanced or Gameboy SP
- mobile telephone.

These are called video games and need to be cabled into a monitor or TV so that the user can interact with the game. The console is controlled using a games controller which plugs into the front of the console. Each console also has its own disk type. Games from a Playstation made by Sony cannot be used in an X-box or Gamecube. Most games come in CD format. Consoles such as the Playstation can be connected to the Internet. Portable gaming is done either through download from the Internet or by using small portable games which slot into a gaming device. Large virtual reality games have been possible because of the advances in technology. These can be played at arcades and present the user with a realistic experience using special goggles and gloves.

Mobile phones are also used to play games which have been downloaded from the provider network or the Internet.

Basically anywhere that there is a processor and a screen, a game can be played. ICT is used in the games industry to create highly specialised games which have 3-D graphic effects and realistic sound and video. Games are now created which demand highly specified hardware to support them.

Advances in graphics, processing power, game design and complexity mean that the most up-to-date games make games design a few years ago look simplistic in comparison. Technology has facilitated the growth in user expectations with regard to games. We are now accustomed to using highly interactive, 3-D, action packed games. As our expectations grow, the games industry is under pressure to meet them with more impressive gaming environments.

Computer gaming is a top leisure activity and many say that the skills gained from playing games can be transferred to others areas of education and training. Games motivate many people to succeed in attaining levels, for this reason gaming technologies and techniques are being used create more effective learning materials for schools and colleges.

■ The impact of ICT on the video industry

The first analogue video recorders captured pictures using video tape. Digital Video (DV) cameras are now used to record moving pictures. DV is a method of recording movies in digital format onto digital video tape. The movie can then be transferred directly onto a PC or iMAC for editing and enhancing. This is done using either a USB cable connected to the DVout port of the camera and the computer or by using *firewire*. Firewire is a special cable which permits the immediate transfer of digital video onto a computer.

Digital Video can:

- Take digital photographs directly onto DV tape or onto a memory stick for later download onto a computer.
- Be connected to a VHS recorder to download movie footage.
- Allow users to edit video footage and apply video effects using facilities on the camera.
- Can be used as a video camera for video conferencing.

Most DVs record onto a mini DV tape holding about one hour of video footage, around 11 GB of data. Some record onto small CD-ROMS or DVDs.

Analogue video recordings can be converted to digital recordings using a video digitizer. Digital videos produced in this way are not of the same high quality as those shot using a DV camera.

The falling cost of this technology means that more people are able to buy DV cameras. But it is the development of the Digital Versatile Disk and video compression which has made the storage of digital movies much easier. Digital Videos take up a large amount of storage space. A few minutes of video will take up 1 GB of storage space. In order to be edited the video must be transferred to the computer. Once edited it must be compressed before it is transferred onto a DVD which has a storage capacity of about 17 GB. A DVD player has a decoder which can uncompress data as we watch it. These advances in technology have resulted in the widespread use of DVDs and DVD players.

DVD technology has been used by the film industry in the distribution of films. All new movies are distributed on DVD. Movies on DVD have been compressed using MPEG2 format and provide significant advantages for users.

The advantages of using DVD

- The picture and sound are of a much higher quality. It is more like going to the cinema.
- DVDs have an onscreen menu allowing the user to select which frame or scene they wish to view. The scenes do not have to be viewed in order.
- DVDs provide subtitles in different languages.
- DVDs usually have additional features such as games associated with the movie or extra information about how the movie was made.
- DVD players can be used to play audio CDs.

DVD players are used in many homes and cost less than £100. Video games are also being distributed on DVD for use on home DVD players.

■ The impact of ICT on shopping

ICT has had a number of effects on how we do our shopping. Most people buying products now make use of credit or debit cards and no cash transaction takes place. Money is transferred using EFT (Electronic Funds Transfer). Credit and debit cards make use of the new *chip and PIN* technology. Signatures will no longer be required at the POS (Point of Sale). The customer enters a PIN (Personal Identification Number) and funds are transferred from their account to the shops account in seconds via the communications links. This technology has been introduced to cut down on credit card fraud. Special new computer systems have been installed in large supermarkets to enable the *chip and PIN* system to be used.

E-commerce is the buying and selling of goods on the World Wide Web. It has had a major effect on shopping. Consumers using the Internet for shopping have access to all the major stores 24 hours a day. Tesco have one of the most successful online shopping stores. On this website it is possible to shop for groceries and book a delivery slot. Shoppers can access products bought on previous shopping trips through *My Favourites*. The products are paid for by credit or debit card and the goods are delivered to the door.

What are the advantages of shopping like this?

Advantages for the consumer:

- Shopping can be done from the comfort of your own home 24 hours a day, 7 days a week. This is helpful for busy people and those with young children who may find it difficult to visit the supermarket or shop.
- Elderly and disabled people can shop for heavy items and have them delivered without the inconvenience of visiting the store.
- Shoppers can use a wider variety of stores giving them a greater choice of items. The stores can be anywhere in the world.
- Customers are looking at a larger range of shops so shops may have to be competitive in their pricing to attract customers.

Advantages for the company:

- The website is open 24/7 and requires few personnel. Checkout operators are not required.
- The website can be accessed from anywhere in the world so the company has the chance of getting more customers.
- If a small company sets up an e-commerce site, it can trade without the need to rent large city centre premises.

Concerns for the consumer:

- Not all consumers may have access to a computer or the Internet.
- Not all consumers have the necessary skills to navigate the Internet.
- There is the possibility of being defrauded if the website is not secure.
- Not all websites are authentic. Bogus websites could con customers into giving valuable information or credit card details.
- Orders made on websites can be harder to rectify if an error is made.

- On authentic websites credit card details can be intercepted.
- Once personal data is submitted to a website it may be intercepted and used for different purposes.

What is a secure website?

The biggest concern most people have about buying online is security. Secure websites use an Internet protocol called Secure Socket Layers (SSL) to protect credit card data. This performs several important things in the background. Data is encrypted or scrambled before being sent from your computer to the server. This means that hackers will not be able to get at your details. The data is then reconstructed when it reaches the company's server. Customers are at significantly more risk of fraud if they give their credit card to a retailer to swipe outside of their view, for example at a restaurant.

Encryption is a mathematical process which uses formulae to scramble data before it is transmitted. In most cases encryption involves a key. The sender uses a secret key to encrypt the data and the receiver uses a private key to unscramble or decrypt the data.

Secure Electronic Transaction (SET) is a protocol co-owned by Visa and Mastercard designed to make online purchases much more secure for credit card users. SET makes use of a two-stage authentication process using digital signatures and digital certificates. The company sends the consumer a digital signature which confirms the company's identity. When sent the account details to pay for goods, customers send a digital signature which allows the bank to confirm the customer's identity. A digital certificate sent by the bank will confirm the customer's identity and ability to pay.

Definition of terms associated with SET

Term	Definition
Digital certificate	An electronic identification that confirms that the user is an authentic person. A bank will issue this certificate which contains information about the user.
Digital signature	A code that guarantees a sender's identity. If an unauthorized person decrypts it, the digital signature will be altered. This means that the recipient will recognise that the code has been decrypted.

An easy way to see if the page you are on is secure is the closed padlock displayed at the bottom of most browsers. Additionally, the address of the website that you are visiting (displayed in the address bar of your browser) will change to start with https://.

Computers and the law

The widespread use of computers to hold and process personal information has prompted the Government to design laws to deal with the illegal use of computers, digital information and software. The laws are:

- Computer Misuse Act of 1990
- The Copyright Designs and Patents Act of 1988
- The Data Protection Act.

■ Computer Misuse Act

As general computer usage grew during the 1970s and 1980s, so did the incidence of people using computers for criminal purposes, for example accessing and amending data in bank accounts. New digital crimes emerged.

Hacking

Hacking can be defined as intentionally accessing a computer system without consent. Hackers are people who gain unauthorized entry to a computer system. Hacking is usually done remotely using telephone lines. Most people involved in this process are motivated to *beat the system*.

Planting of viruses

A virus can be defined as a program that has been designed to damage the operation of a computer automatically.

There are many viruses around but generally they tend to destroy user files, display annoying messages or graphics or store themselves as *hidden* files on your hard drive. Some viruses are set to trigger on certain dates so you may not know you have it until the day it does the damage.

This prompted a new government law called the **Computer Misuse Act (1990)**.

Brief overview of the principles of the Computer Misuse Act

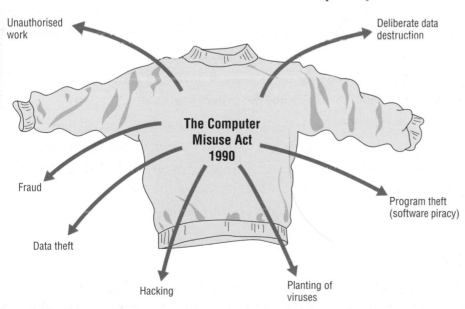

Unauthorised work

Deliberate data destruction

The Computer Misuse Act 1990

Fraud

Data theft

Hacking

Planting of viruses

Program theft (software piracy)

▲ The Computer Misuse Act is designed to prevent many wrongdoings

This law deals with problems involving hacking, viruses and other nuisances by making it illegal to:

- plant viruses in a computer system deliberately
- gain unauthorised access to a computer system
- commit crimes like fraud using a computer, for example using a computer to transfer money between bogus bank accounts to save on tax payment
- use a company's computer for personal purposes without permission.

■ Copyright legislation – The Copyright Designs and Patents Act

This law was designed to protect the property rights of people and organisations that create and produce material based on original ideas. Material of this kind, sometimes referred to as *intellectual property*, includes books, articles, music, films, software, paintings and other individual inventions. The law gives the owner of the material or idea the right to prevent it being circulated or copied. Consider the cost involved in making and distributing a music CD. Artists depend on the revenue made from the sales of the CD. If the CD is copied by everyone rather than bought, the artists will receive no money and will be unable to pay off the costs incurred during production. This is not fair and is now illegal and is referred to as *piracy*. Piracy usually involves the illegal copying or distribution of someone else's work. There are other areas where copyright can be breached, for example:

- photocopying pages from a text book and distributing them without the author's permission
- using photographs from a website or text book without permission
- copying films on DVD and distributing them
- using music in advertisements or presentations without the composer's permission
- presenting someone else's material or ideas as your own.

From a digital and ICT viewpoint, there are *four main areas* where legislation is needed:

- software piracy, which includes the illegal copying or downloading of software.
- the *theft* by one company of the ideas and methods of other ICT companies
- the use of ICT (including the Internet) to copy or download material such as music, video or text-based files, thus avoiding the price of purchase
- using unlicensed software.

What is software piracy?

Software piracy takes two main forms:

- individual users borrowing CDs or DVDs or using the Internet to copy a piece of software to their own computers
- professional criminals making copies in bulk and selling them through illegal outlets.

The software industry believes that there are three negative effects of this piracy:

- it results in higher prices for those customers who are buying software legally
- it discourages software houses from being innovative
- it means that artists and creators are not getting the correct and rightful income from the sales of their product.

What is software licensing?

Most organisations run their computers on networks. When they buy a piece of software, they also purchase a licence for a certain number of users. They are then legally permitted to distribute the software for a fixed number of users at any one time. If the organisation wants more users to access the program, then they have to pay for more licences. Some organisations, however, do not do this. They distribute the software over the network with no regard for how many licences they have or, indeed, whether they have a licence at all. Many software producers such as Microsoft have helped fund an organisation known as FAST (The Federation Against Software Theft) to protect against illegal use of their software.

■ Data Protection Act

Background

As more information was stored on computers, much of it was personal data about individuals. This meant that there was a need to control what was stored in the interests of protecting individuals. The digital nature of the information meant that it was easily distributed. Internet technology meant that data could be sent anywhere in the world in seconds. Data security and privacy became an important issue for those companies and organisations holding personal data.

People became concerned that data about them was being shared between companies without their permission. Another major concern was that personal data about them was being accessed by people who could misuse it. Personal data is a very sensitive area for most people.

What is personal data?

Personal data is data about an individual which they consider to be private. If someone answers a questionnaire or fills out a form for a company, they may not want the information to be shared with other companies. Before the Data Protection Act companies could have shared the information. Most forms now have a box included which can be ticked to stop them sharing information about the person filling out the form.

Most people accept that there is data held about people in areas like:

- medical records
- school or college records
- criminal records
- birth, death and marriage records
- census records
- inland revenue records
- employee records.

However, data about us is collected all the time. Sometimes we may not even be aware of it.

- Supermarkets use loyalty cards to collect data about our shopping habits and use it to inform their stock, marketing and advertising departments.
- CCIT cameras monitor the activity of people in many town centres.
- Mobile phones transmit your location at any point in time.
- Each use of a credit or debit card gives banks and credit card companies information on your shopping patterns, and location.
- When using the internet personal computers can transmit an IP (Internet Protocol) address which can give details about location. Cookies can also be downloaded which record activity on the Internet.

▷ Means by which personal information is collected

Internet 'cookies', without you knowing, record details of the web sites you have visited

Cameras at ports record the registration numbers of vehicles entering or leaving the country

ATM (cash dispensers) record transaction details (date, time, location, amount withdrawn, etc). Some will secretly take your photograph

Loyalty cards and credit cards link you to the purchases you make

When mobile phones are switched on, their whereabouts can be located fairly accurately

If a company collects data about people we expect the information to be used correctly and stored securely. This is now a legal requirement demanded by the Data Protection Act.

The Data Protection Act demands that those collecting and using data about others take responsibility for it. There are eight principles which companies must agree to. Personal data should:

- be processed fairly and lawfully with the consent of the data subject
- be used for the specified purpose only
- be adequate and relevant for its intended purpose
- be accurate and up to date
- not be kept for longer than necessary
- be processed in accordance with the rights of the data subject
- be held securely, with no unauthorised access
- not be transferred outside the EU.

Definitions of terms used within the Data Protection Act

Term	Definition
Personal data	Concerns a living person who can be identified from the data
Data subject	The individual who is the subject of the personal data
The data commissioner	Responsible for enforcing the Act Promoting good practice from those people responsible for processing personal data Making the general public aware of their rights under the Act
The data controller	The person in a company who is responsible for controlling the way in which personal data is processed

The data subject:

- has the right to view data held about them; sometimes they may have to pay a fee and send a letter requesting this
- has the right to have the data explained if they do not understand it
- can be denied access to information if it is being used for crime detection/prevention, or for tax purposes.

The data controller:

- must notify the data commissioner of their intention to store data
- must specify the security in place to protect the data from unauthorised access.

Failure to abide by these two items will result in prosecution of the organisation.

Questions for C3

1 Expand the following acronyms.

Acronym	Expand
CD-ROM	
CD	
LAN	
WAN	
DVD	
MIDI	
RSI	
ELF (higher tier only)	
MIDI	
MPEG	
MP3	
POS	
EFT	
FAST	
SET (higher tier only)	

2 ICT has affected many aspects of our everyday lives. Prepare a multimedia presentation which will show new technology is used in:

Education
Employment

Higher Tier Extension   Include a slide which describes how people's work patterns have changed. Your presentation should include a master slide with navigation buttons.

3 Full course only question.

A company is setting up a new computer resource room for office workers. The room will hold 15 people who work from 9am to 5pm each day. You have been asked to inform the company about their Health and Safety responsibilities.

Construct a report which you will give to management outlining what should be considered under health and safety. Your report should be no more than 250 words.

Higher Tier Extension   Add to your report a section on possible injuries which can be caused by poor ergonomics.

4 Your grandparents have asked you to tell them about the new music and video technologies. Make a simple leaflet which will describe what the technologies do.

Higher Tier Extension Include in your leaflet a list of the advantages of using this new technology.

5 a) What is teleworking?
  b) What are the advantages for an employee who undertakes teleworking?
  c) What are the disadvantages for an employee who undertakes teleworking?

Higher Tier Extension d) What equipment is required in order for a person to undertake teleworking.
  e) What are the advantages and disadvantages to a company when it makes use of teleworkers.

6 You have been asked by a teacher to show her how to do online shopping. Produce a guide which will:
  a) Explain what online shopping is.
  b) Explain the advantages of online shopping.
  c) Take her to the Tesco website.

Higher Tier Extension d) Show her some of the features of the website.
  e) Let her register as an online shopper.

Full Course only extension f) Identify how transactions are kept secure on the Internet.

7 State the purpose of each of the following Laws
  The Data Protection Act
  The Copyright Designs and Patens Act
  The Computer Misuse Act

8 a) Explain what is meant by Personal Data.
  b) State the eight principles of the Data Protection Act.

Higher Extension Task c) What is the role of the following in connection with the Data Protection Act.
  The data subject
  The data controller
  The data commissioner

9 The use of credit cards in online shopping causes some shoppers concern. There are security measures which can be taken.
  a) What is a secure website?
  b) How can a secure website be identified?
  c) What kind of fraud could occur if a website is not secure?

Higher Tier Extension d) How can encryption be used to ensure that credit card transactions are secure.
  e) What are *digital signatures* and *digital certificates* and what is their role in secure electronic transactions.

Advice on assessment

Guidance hints and tips for the GCSE ICT examination

The CCEA GCSE ICT is available in two forms:
- The Short Course
- The Full Course

Course	Examination	Coursework*
Full Course Foundation	Paper 1 Foundation – 1½ hours Worth 20% of overall marks Paper 2 Foundation – 1 hour Worth 20% of overall marks	Assignments A1 – A3 Assignments B1 – B3 Worth 60% of overall marks
Full Course Higher	Paper 1 Higher – 1½ hours Worth 20% of overall marks Paper 2 Higher – 1 hour Worth 20% of overall marks	Assignments A1 – A3 Assignments B1 – B3 Worth 60% of overall marks
Short Course Foundation	Paper 1 Foundation – 1½ hours Worth 40% of overall marks	ONE assignment from A1 – A3 Assignments B1 – B3 Worth 60% of overall marks
Short Course Higher	Paper 1 Higher – 1½ hours Worth 40% of overall marks	ONE Assignment from A1 – A3 Assignments B1 – B3 Worth 60% of overall marks

Coursework

The coursework element is worth 60% of the overall qualification marks. (*Coursework assignments can be downloaded from www.ccea.org.uk).

Tip	Reason
Ensure you have a copy of the assignment brief and the mark scheme. You can download this from www.ccea.org.uk.	You will be able to see how much each assignment is worth and how to gain as many marks as possible
Assignments A1 – A3 are all worth 19 marks. Part of the marks are allocated for a report on the assignment. Use a spell checker and get someone to proofread your report.	This will help the overall quality of the report and may gain you extra marks for Quality of Written Communication (QWC).
Make use of labelled screen shots to explain the features of software which you have used.	Pictures can be easier to understand than a paragraph of text. You may find it easier to label a screen shot than to explain what you have done.
Assignment B2 is worth 18 marks, accuracy here can achieve full marks.	
Store your completed assignments in hard copy and also electronically. Keep a note of where you have stored them and what filenames you have used.	You can refer to the assignments and make any changes necessary if you have an electronic copy.

Tip (continued)	Reason (continued)
Remember that your choice of topic for Assignments A1, A2, A3 and B1 is up to you. You can use a topic you have prepared for another subject as a basis for your coursework.	You can build on work already started and may be able to produce a better product.
Minor Points: ● Good presentation of coursework makes it easier to mark. ● Before submitting an assignment check off the requirements on the mark scheme. ● All assignments should be neatly presented with a list of contents and page numbers. ● Your teacher will tell you how they want you to submit the assignments. If you are not sure ASK. One way might be to submit each assignment in a project folder.	

Examination

The examination element is worth 40% of the overall marks.

Paper 1

All pupils take this paper. If you are a foundation level pupil you will do the foundation paper. The paper normally has a multiple-choice question at the beginning. The question paper may then have up to 15 more questions.

Paper 2

Only those pupils following the Full Course specification take this paper. It lasts for 1 hour and normally contains about 12 questions with a long question at the end.

Preparing for the examination

Tip	Reason
● Always make sure you have a copy of the specification. You can get this at www.ccea.org.uk. ● Note that the specification is divided up into three sections and plan your revision using this fact.	This will let you see the content of the course and you can identify keywords and acronyms.
● Use a notebook or create a document which contains all of the acronyms in each section, together with their meaning. Call this your glossary.	If you look at each paper there are quite a lot of acronyms to be explained. This is an easy place to start revising.

Tip (continued)	Reason (continued)
● Using this book, record in the glossary, the keywords identified at the top of each section together with a definition.	Sometimes you are asked to explain the meaning of keywords in the examination.
● Paper 1 is common to both the Short and the Full Courses. When preparing a revision list prioritise the topics that are on the Short Course Specification. You can get this at www.ccea.org.uk.	Your revision strategy will be targeted and more effective.
● Revise the skills you have learned. Look for online exercises that will help you revise your practical skills. Look on the website for the book to find some useful links. ● Revise software by identifying the main functions and advanced features.	You will be asked questions about section C1. Your coursework has been developed over a period of time and you may forget about the functions of the software you have studied.
● Use a spider diagram to help you with your revision. Look on the website for the book to find some examples of spider diagrams.	This gives you a picture of what you are learning and for some people might be easier to remember.
● Become familiar with the structure of the examination. You can buy past examination papers and mark schemes from CCEA. Your teacher can also get them for you.	Familiar layout will help you settle quickly during the examination and may improve your performance. Also some questions on past papers may appear again.
Note that the paper is laid out as follows:	
● 1 mark questions have one line for a response.	The examiner will expect you to make one relevant point to gain the mark.
● 2 mark questions have two or three lines for a response.	The examiner will expect you to make two relevant points in your response to gain full marks.
● 3 mark questions have three or four lines for response. There are fewer of these questions.	The examiner will expect you to make three relevant points in your response to gain full marks.
● The long question on Paper 2 is usually worth up to 8 marks.	Make sure you make up to eight different relevant points; one for each mark allocated.

2004 Higher Level GCSE ICT papers

Section C1

1 A company keeps a database with two tables. The tables are Supplier and Part. The structure of the tables can be seen to here:

Below is some data from each of the tables:

Supplier Table	Part Table
Supplier Code	Part Number
Supplier Name	Supplier Code
Street	Description
Area	Cost Price
Town	Selling Price
Postcode	In Stock
Telephone	On Order

Part Table

Part Number	Supplier Code	Description	CostPrice	SellingPrice	InStock	OnOrder
DEC001	BLA100	Twin Tip Deck	£6.65	£8.50	0	Yes

Supplier Code	Supplier Name	Street	Area	Town	Postcode	Telephone
BLA100	Back & Sons	23 Long Road	Bangor	Co. Down	BT22 0EU	028000706050

a) Suggest key fields for each of the two tables. (2 marks)

b) The files are held in a relational database. Explain the term **Relational Database**. (2 marks)

c) Explain why the Supplier Code is in the Part Table. (2 marks)

d) Suggest data types for the following fields: Supplier Code, Telephone, CostPrice, InStock.

Higher Tier Only

e) A data capture form has been created using a wizard in the database package.
   (i) What is a wizard? (2 marks)
   (ii) Explain the purpose of a data capture form. (2 marks)
   (iii) List two other features provided by a database that can help users to provide meaningful and useful information. (2 marks)

(CCEA 2004)

2 Browser software can be used to view pages across the Internet.
   a) Name two web browsers. (2 marks)
   b) Users can return to their selected home page by clicking on the icon similar to the one shown. Name four other icons you would expect to find on a browser menu bar. (4 marks)

Higher Tier Only

   c) the web address of the CCEA "ICT" homepage is http://www.ccea.org.uk/ict/. Explain what each of the following mean: http, www, .org.

Section C2

3 This diagram shows the properties of Joan's hard disk on her PC.
   a) How big is Joan's hard disk? (1 mark)

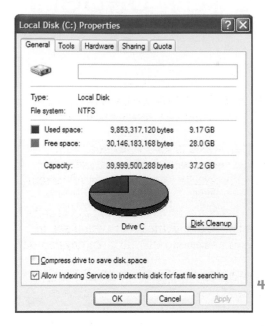

b) Joan wishes to keep a backup copy of the contents of the entire hard disk.
   (i) Which *storage media* would you recommend to hold the contents of her hard disk? (1 mark)
   (ii) What is the purpose of keeping backup copies of any files? (2 marks)

c) Joan has 3 floppy disks containing coursework for different subjects. What's the maximum amount of information she can store *on a single* floppy disk? (1 mark)

d) Joan has completed her geography coursework and finds that she cannot fit it all on to one floppy disk to bring it to school for printing. Describe one way in which Joan could get her work onto the school system. (2 marks)

e) Joan has made use of both **optical** and **magnetic** storage media. Give **one** example of each. (2 marks)

(Adapted from CCEA 2004)

4 A student has bought a new multimedia PC to assist her in the preparation of coursework.
   a) List **two** facilities you would expect to find in a Multimedia PC. (2 marks)
   b) Volatile and non-volatile **memory** exist on this PC, and are available in the form of ROM, RAM, and CACHE. State whether each is volatile or non-volatile and give its typical storage capacity. (6 marks)
   c) Explain how Cache memory is used in a computer system. (2 marks)
   d) The Multimedia PC comes with Microsoft Windows 2000 and Microsoft Office 2000 pre-installed. Microsoft Windows is an operating system with a GUI.
      (i) What do the letters GUI represent? (1 mark)
      (ii) State two ways that the GUI operating system is helpful to a user who has not used a computer before. (2 marks)
      (iii) List three of the main functions of an operating system. (3 marks)

Section C3

5 Many people worry about privacy issues when using the Internet. Certain measures are in place to provide protection for users. How do the following provide protection from users: Digital signatures, SET, Encryption? (6 marks)

6 New technologies have had a major impact on our lifestyles. There have been many changes in the music, leisure and entertainment industries.
   a) Give four examples of how new technology has made changes to the music, entertainment and leisure industries. (3 marks)
   b) Information and communication technology (ICT), is also changing the way in which we learn. Describe how each of the following new technologies might be used to support teaching and learning: CD ROM, Intranet, Internet, Email. (6 marks)

Glossary

ACTUATOR   A device that can be connected to a computer to allow communication between a machine and a computer. The signals from the computer causes movement, such as a motor in a washing machine

ADSL   Asymetric Digital Subscriber Line. A high bandwidth digital line which connects to the Internet.

ARITHMETIC AND LOGIC UNIT   This is part of the CPU were calculations are carried out and logical decisions are made.

ASCII   American Standard Code for Information Interchange. A widely used standard for encoding documents on computers. Each symbol on the keyboard has a specific code. For example the letter "A" has the code 65.

BACKUP   A copy of data which is held at a safe location and used if the original file becomes lost or damaged.

BANDWIDTH   A measurement, usually in megabits per second or kilobits per second, which states the rate at which data travels along a communications line. The higher the bandwidth the quicker data will travel along the line.

BARCODE   A pattern of thick and thin vertical lines used to store data about products. These patterns can be read directly into the computer by a barcode reader.

BATCH PROCESSING   This involves collecting data over a period of time (as a batch) and then processing this data collectively at a convenient time such as night time. The batch is held in a transaction file, and after processing the master file is updated.

BOOTING-UP PROGRAM   This program is used to start the machine by loading the operating system into the main memory from the hard disk. This is done each time the machine is switched on

CACHE MEMORY   This is part of the computers main memory used to store frequently accessed data values such as web addresses to allow for increased access speeds.

CHARACTER   A character is a letter, or a digit, or a punctuation mark, or a symbol, or a control code that can be stored by a computer. Each character is stored in digital format usually referred to as a byte.

CHECK DIGIT   A digit added to the beginning or end of a number to verify that the number entered is an authentic code. For example ISBNs on books have a check digit added to the end. The reading computer calculates the checks digit, if it matches the check digit at the end of the ISBN then it is a valid ISBN.

COMPUTER MISUSE ACT   A law which is designed to prevent people from using computers to perform illegal acts.

CONTROL KEY   This key is labelled Ctrl and when pressed with another key(s) performs an instruction, such as Ctrl+P will print the contents of your current work.

CONTROL UNIT   This is a part of the CPU that controls and co-ordinates all the activities that take place in the processor such as moving instructions into and out of memory.

COPYRIGHT DESIGN AND PATENTS ACT 1998   A law which is designed to ensure that work created by individuals cannot be widely copied without their consent. This means that it s illegal to copy software or music CDs.

CSV   Comma Separated Variables. Data stored in this format can be used in a spreadsheet or database. The data is held as lines of text. Each item on the line is separated by a comma and could represent a field value in a database or a cell value in a spreadsheet. Each line of text could represent a record in a database or a row in a spreadsheet.

CURSOR KEY   These keys are known as the "arrow keys" and are used to control the cursor (or I bar) on the screen. The cursor is recognised as the vertical flashing I bar on the screen.

DATA   Unprocessed facts and figures which on their own have no meaning. Data is entered into a computer and processed, it then becomes information.

DATABASE   A collection of data which is stored in a structure way, usually made up of fields and records.

DATA BUS   A set of wires used to transfer data from one component of a computer to another component. Data buses are embedded into the microprocessor circuit boards.

DATA CAPTURE   The way in which data from a source is entered into a computer.

DATA COMPRESSION   Reducing the size of a file by using special software such as WinZip. Compressed data has to be decompressed before it can be used.

DATA INTEGRITY   The validity or integrity of data can be affected by human error during data entry, software bugs, hardware malfunctions. Data is most reliable when integrity is high.

DATA LOGGING   Capturing data at regular intervals by a device such as a sensor. It is then stored for analysing at a later time.

DATA PROTECTION ACT   A law which is designed to ensure that data held about people on computer or paper is correct, managed properly and stored securely.

DATA REDUNDANCY   If data is repeated or stored more than once in a database system then it is called redundant data. Relational databases minimise data redundancy.

DATA SECURITY   Data must be kept safely and protected from loss through computer crash, corruption, viruses, hackers and physical threats.

DATA VALIDATION   A process whereby the computer checks data against a set of predefined rules ensuring it is correct. Different validation checks are available such as a range check or a character length check.

DATA VERIFICATION   A process to check that data has been entered correctly from a source document. There are two methods of verification available: Double entry and visual checking.

DIGITAL DATA   Data in a format known as binary which consists of two digits: 0 and 1. These digits are known as BITs (Binary digITs) and characters tend to be represented by eight bits in a format known as ASCII codes.

DIGITAL SIGNATURE   A digital code which is attached to an electronic message and uniquely identifies and authenticates the sender.

DIGITAL TELEVISION   The transmission of television signals in digital format. Both sound and picture can be transmitted together.

DISK FORMATTING   This is a stage of preparing a disk so as it can be read from and written to by a given computer. Formatting involves creating tracks and sectors for data storing and retrieval.

DVD   Digital Versatile Disk. Optical disc which has a storage capacity of 4.7 Gigabytes and can hold a full movie. A double sided–double layered DVD has a storage capacity of 17 Gigabytes.

E-COMMERCE   This is defined as a means of conducting business transactions over electronic networks. It includes activities such as online shopping and online banking.

EMAIL   Electronic mail. A tool for sending and receiving messages electronically across a network of computers. This allows users to send messages and file attachments to other users on a network by using a system of electronic mailboxes. Mail that is sent is normally received immediately. To send and receive emails each user needs an email address.

ENCRYPTION   A way of encoding data before transmitting it on a network. Data is encoded by the sending computer using a software encoding key and sent along the communications line. The data can only be decoded by the receiving computer if it has the decoding key. This keeps data secure whilst it is being transmitted between computers. It is used on the Internet for credit card transactions to ensure that the user's credit card number is not detected.

EXPERT SYSTEM   This is a computer system that attempts to emulate a human. It involves collecting information from all the human experts in a given area and creating a knowledge base and rules. This in turn can be accessed by a user in the form of querying the knowledge base looking for a solution to a problem. It is widely used in the field of medicine.

EXTERNAL MEMORY   This refers to memory devices that are connected to a computer system but are not integrated such as floppy disk drives, hard drives and CD drives. These types of memories are used to store data permanently and any data that is not currently being used.

FAX   Facsimile. A device which is used to transfer paper based information along telephone lines.

FEEDBACK   This is a situation when an output can influence the next input(s). It normally occurs in real time processing such as when data from sensors are input to a controlling program and when processed the output can contribute to selecting the next input. For example in a home heating system the feedback could be the house is too warm, therefore turn off the heating.

FILE ARCHIVE   These are files that are no longer active in that data will not be added, deleted or changed. There only purpose is to act as a reference to old data. They are sometimes called reference files.

FILE BACKUP   Keeping copies of files in a separate source in case anything happens to the original copies through theft or corruption. Normally files backups take place on a regular basis and are stored on a medium such as magnetic tape.

FILE RECOVERY   This is a process of restoring a file once it is found to contain incorrect data. This normally involves using a transaction file to update a master file. A recovery log is then kept of the generations of master and transaction files to be used in the event of file corruption.

FILE UPDATING   This involves altering an existing data item already written to a file. Therefore after a file update the data should be the most recent version.

FUNCTION KEY   These keys are labelled with F followed by a number usually found on the top row of a QWERTY keyboard. They are programmed to carry out a task and act as a shortcut to performing this task as it only requires the user to press the relevant function key.

HACKING   Gaining unauthorised access to a computer system.

HARD COPY   A permanent copy of information usually in the form of a printout.

HOT KEY   This is known as a shortcut key and can also be a combination of keys. When these are pressed a task will be carried out. They are designed for use by experienced users as an alterative to using a mouse and menus.

HTML   HyperText Markup Language. The language used to construct webpages. Most website development packages generate HTML.

INFORMATION   Data which has been processed and is presented in a way which is meaningful to users.

INTERNAL MEMORY   This is the memory that is inside the CPU and is usually chip based memory. RAM and ROM are examples of internal memory.

INTERNET   A network of computer networks linked together using a variety of communications technologies such as cables and wireless transmission. The computers and cables constitute the Internet.

INTERNET FILTERING   A way of checking websites to ensure that the content is suitable for viewing. If the website is not suitable it will not be allowed through the Internet filter.

INTRANET   A website which is only available to employees or members of an organisation, school or college. The website is usually stored on a file server which belongs to the organisation. Members can access the website from within the local area network and in some cases can log on to the website from home. Access to the website is restricted to those people who belong to the organisation.

ISDN   Integrated Services Digital Network. An Internet connection which requires to telephone lines and has a bandwidth of 64 to 128 kilobits per second.

ISP   Internet Service Provider. A company which provides a user with a connection to the Internet. ISPs usually give email and web space to their users. An ISP is necessary to enable connection to the Internet.

LAN   Local Area Network. Computers linked together using cables or wireless technology, within one building or over a small geographic area.

MAGNETIC STRIPE   This is an integral part of a plastic card such as a credit card. On this tape data can be stored and read by a magnetic stripe reader.

MAIN MEMORY   This is the memory were data and instructions are held for use by the CPU. It is sometimes called the immediate access memory.

MASTER FILE   The main file to store data in a computer system. A transaction file is used to update a master file in a given application.

MIDI   Musical Instrument Digital Interface. The standard used when recording and playing back music on digital synthesisers.

MODELLING   Creating a set of rules that can simulate a real–life situation done by a computer. An important feature of modelling is the ability to carry out what..if situations or making predictions.

MP3   An MPEG standard used to transmit music digitally across the Internet.

MPEG   Moving Pictures Experts Group. A standard developed by this group, used to compress digital video.

MULTIMEDIA   The combination of text, graphics, voice, video and sound to produce a presentation. Since multimedia presentations require vast amounts of storage they are normally stored on optical discs.

OCR   Optical Character Recognition – A method of capturing data directly from a sheet of paper. Input is done using a special machine which can read the typed or handwritten characters from the page. The characters are then converted to digital characters which the computer can understand. A flatbed scanner can read a typed document and produce a digital version which can be edited on the computer. This is a form of Optical Character Recognition.

OMISSION ERROR   When keying data into a computer system one or more characters may have been left out. For example 12345 is keyed as 1245 hence an omission error

OMR   Optical Mark Recognition – A method of capturing data which has been recorded as marks on a sheet of paper. The marks are read from the form and are converted into digital data. Multiple choice tests and questionnaires can be processed using this technology.

ONLINE   When two devices are connected to receive or transmit information they are described as being online. This could be a computer and a printer. The term is normally associated with the Internet.

PERIPHERAL DEVICE   A hardware component connected to the computer. These can be categorised into input devices, output devices and storage devices. In other words all the components excluding the CPU.

PIXEL   The smallest area on a VDU that can be edited such as changing the colour. A picture is made up of pixels. The greater the amount of pixels the higher the resolution, hence a better quality image.

PRESENCE CHECK   A validation check to ensure that data being entered into the computer system is present, that is no fields are left blank. This type of check is used on an online form where some details are marked with an asterisk (*). The user cannot submit the form until all of the data in these fields is present.

PROTOCOL   A set of rules which govern the way in which data is transmitted between computers on a network.

PSTN   Public Switched Telephone Network. The voice oriented telephone network. This provides the basic infrastructure for much of the Internet.

RANDOM ACCESS   This is the ability to access data directly. It is sometimes referred to as direct access. Random access is used to read and write to magnetic disks as the order of files on the medium is not sequential. Magnetic tapes use sequential access.

RANDOM ACCESS MEMORY   Sometimes referred to as the main memory of a computer system. It is used to store the current programs and data required by the user. When a computer is switched on the operating system is loaded from the hard drive into RAM. Since the contents of RAM can change it is described as being volatile.

RANGE CHECK   A validation check to ensure that data being entered into the computer system is within an acceptable range, usually defined by the system designers. For example if a student's age was to be entered the acceptable range might be 11–65. The range check would not allow data outside of this range to be entered.

READ ONLY MEMORY (ROM)   A form of computer memory where the contents can be read but not changed. Even when the power of the computer is switched off, the contents remain. The bootstrap program to start the computer is stored in ROM.

RELATIONAL DATABASE   A collection of data stored in a structured way. The database is made up of tables of data. A table contains records. Each record is made up of fields. The tables are linked together using common fields, this allows efficient searching and storage of data

RESOLUTION   This measures the quality of an image in pixels. It is the total number of pixels displayed horizontally and vertically by a visual display unit. The resolution of VDUs can vary.

ROUTER   A device which connects two or more networks together. It can work out the best route for data to travel between computers. A router is used to link a local area network to the Internet. The router will receive data from the Internet and send it on the best route along the network to the requesting computer.

RSI   Repetitive Strain Injury. An injury which occurs as a result of using the same muscles over and over again. This can be common in a computer user who does not have the correct equipment to prevent this.

RTF   Rich Text Format. A standardised way of storing a document and its formatting so that it can be transferred to different word-proccesing applications while retaining the original formatting.

SEARCH ENGINE   A program which allows a user to search through the network of computers on the Internet to find information. Different search engines will return different results for the same search criteria because they search different computers for the information. Examples of search engines are Yahoo! and Google.

SENSOR   An electronic component that converts energy from one source to another to be understood by a computer system.

SERIAL ACCESS   A complete list of files examined by looking at each one in turn until the file you are looking for is found. This type of access is used with magnetic tape.

SET   Secure Electronic Transaction. A standard that enables secure credit card transactions on the Internet. SET has been accepted by all of the major credit card companies. SET allows credit card users to make purchases without the company viewing their credit card number.

SHIFT KEY   On a keyboard each key normally consists of two characters, such as a small letter (lowercase) and a capital letter (uppercase). The shift key allows the user to toggle between the two characters.

SIMULATION   A computer program used to model a real-life situation and associated behaviour, such as an aircraft cockpit were the model would be built based on a variety of possible situations that may be experienced by pilots.

SMART CARD   A plastic card such as a bank card that contains a microchip and a built-in memory. The memory is bigger than the memory available on a magnetic stripe

SOFT COPY   This is a non-permanent copy of text or graphical information displayed on a VDU or it could be in the form of spoken word through speakers.

TELECONFERENCING   A meeting held between people who are at a distance from each other using communications technology such as the Internet and videocameras.

TELEPRESENCE   This term is used in medicine to describe a situation of creating a "virtual patient" to be used by surgeons to practise an operation.

TELEWORKING   Working from home using technology such as email and teleconferencing, to communicate with the office rather than travelling to work.

TRACKS AND SECTORS   When a disk is formatted it will contain tracks and sectors. Tracks are circular areas on a storage medium such a floppy disk used for storing data on. Sectors are cross sections of tracks so when a file is stored it will contain both a track and a sector reference.

TRANSACTION FILE   These store new records, updates for existing records or records to be deleted from a master file.

TRANSCRIPTION ERROR   This is an error that is created when transferring data from one source to another source. Typically this may involve keying in incorrect data from a source document into a word-processing package.

TRANSPOSITION ERROR   An error that occurs when the data is keyed in and characters swap places, for example the number 12345 is keyed in as 12435

TYPE CHECK   A validation check to ensure that data being entered into the computer system is of the correct type. Data types include text (alphanumeric), numeric (integer, long integer, byte), date, yes/no (Boolean).

URL   Uniform Resource Locator. A web address which when typed into the address bar of a browser will take the user to a website. An example of a URL is *www.ccea.org.uk*

VALIDATION   A way of ensuring that only correct data will be entered into the system. Data is checked to ensure it is present, of the right type, in the correct range and of the correct length.

VERIFICATION   A way of checking that data has been entered into the computer system accurately. Data can be entered into the computer system twice by two different users. The data is verified by checking that

the two sets of data match, if they don't then one of the users has made an error when entering the data. Proof reading is another method of verification.

VIRTUAL REALITY   A computer simulated world. It involves computer controlled graphics to generate realistic scenes which the user can interact with.

VIRUS   A program which has been designed to damaged a computer system. It can be spread from one computer to another through floppy disks, Zip disks or memory sticks. They can also be sent by email.

VOICE MAIL   This is a spoken word version of email. It is similar to a message left on an answering machine except the message is stored on a computer.

WAN   Wide Area Network. Computers linked together using cables and wireless or satelite technology, over a large geographic area. The Internet is a WAN.

WAP   Wireless Applications Protocol. A standard used for communicating over wireless networks. Some mobile phones are WAP enabled and can access the Internet.

WEB BROWSER   A piece of software which allows the user to look at web pages. Examples of web browsers are Netscape Navigator and Microsoft Internet Explorer.

WORLD WIDE WEB   The information which is held and travels along the Internet. This information is held as web pages or files which can be downloaded. It can be multimedia, for example sound, animation and pictures.

Index

Rewarding Learning

information and communication technology

FOR CCEA GCSE

gerry_lynch
siobhan_matthewson

Hodder Murray

A MEMBER OF THE HODDER HEADLINE GROUP

The Publishers would like to thank the following for permission to reproduce copyright material:

Photo credits
Archos (page 222); Bob Battersby/BDI Images Ltd (pages 182 top left, 192 right); Comstock Images/Getty (page 150); Corbis (pages 131, 132 middle, 136 both, 148, 178, 180 both, 182 all middle images, 195, 196, 214 left); Digifusion (page 181); DVLA (page 142); Hodder Murray (page 214 right); John Walmsley (page 179); Mike Bull (pages 133, 138); Raritan (page 162); Science Photo Library (pages 125, 192 left, 197); Sony (page 183); Steve Connolly (pages 127, 128, 129, 132 left and right, 139, 151, 158 both, 161 both, 177, 182 bottom left, 183, 198, 213, 221); Thomas Cook (page 143).

Every effort has been made to trace all copyright holders, but if any have been inadvertently overlooked the Publishers will be pleased to make the necessary arrangements at the first opportunity.

Although every effort has been made to ensure that website addresses are correct at time of going to press, Hodder Murray cannot be held responsible for the content of any website mentioned in this book. It is sometimes possible to find a relocated web page by typing in the address of the home page for a website in the URL window of your browser.

Orders: please contact Bookpoint Ltd, 130 Milton Park, Abingdon, Oxon OX14 4SB. Telephone: (44) 01235 827720. Fax: (44) 01235 400454. Lines are open 9.00 – 5.00, Monday to Saturday, with a 24-hour message answering service. Visit our website at www.hoddereducation.co.uk

© Siobhan Matthewson, Gerry Lynch 2005
First published in 2005 by
Hodder Murray, an imprint of Hodder Education,
a member of the Hodder Headline Group
338 Euston Road
London NW1 3BH

Impression number   10 9 8 7 6 5 4 3 2
Year   2010 2009 2008 2007 2006

Cover photo Photodisk Collection / Getty Images
Illustrations by Barking Dog Art, Richard Duszczak
Typeset in Boton 12pt by Fakenham Photosetting Ltd, Fakenham, Norfolk
Printed and bound in Italy

A catalogue record for this title is available from the British Library

ISBN-10: 034088309X
ISBN-13: 978 0340 883 099